A Vegan Taste of Italy

A Vegan Taste of Italy

Linda Majzlik

JON CARPENTER

Our books may be ordered from bookshops or (post free in the UK) from
Jon Carpenter Publishing, Alder House, Market Street, Charlbury,
England OX7 3PH

Credit card orders should be phoned or faxed to 01689 870437
or 01608 819117

First published in 2001 by
Jon Carpenter Publishing
Alder House, Market Street, Charlbury, England OX7 3PH
☎ 01608 811969

Reprinted 2011

ISBN 978 1 897766 65 1

Printed in England by CPI Antony Rowe, Chippenham

CONTENTS

INTRODUCTION

E ver since the days of the lavish Roman banquets, Italy has been famous for its excellent cuisine. Two words that aptly describe Italian cookery today are regional and seasonal. Regional, in that each of Italy's twenty regions has its own specialities and distinctive styles of cooking; and seasonal, because most of the fruit and vegetables used are grown in Italy itself. As the climate in parts of Italy is so favourable for horticulture, the country is almost self-sufficient in the production of fruit and vegetables. The cuisine therefore is very dependent on the seasons and each new season is looked forward to and welcomed for its own special produce. The regional differences in cooking style are strongly influenced by history and tradition, with many recipes passed on by word of mouth rather than being written down.

Italy is very much a country of contrasts, with a marked difference between the northern and southern regions which is reflected in cooking styles and the staple ingredients used. The northern regions are more industrial and pros-perous and the land is more fertile, with a favourable growing climate. Rice has been cultivated in Italy since the 15th century, when it was introduced by the Venetians who brought it back from their trading visits to the East. It is grown extensively in the Po Valley and risottos are widely eaten in this part of the country. Corn is also a main crop and polenta, made from maizemeal, is a staple food in the northern regions. Although pasta is eaten throughout Italy the types favoured in the north are the flat varieties, rather than the tubes and shapes which are more popular in the south.

Compared to the affluent north the southern part of Italy is very poor, with less favourable growing conditions. The foods eaten here tend to be simpler and more filling. Vegetables are heavily relied upon and used to make hearty, substantial soups. Bread is very important too and treated with great respect.

Naples is noted for inventing the pizza and also the world famous Italian ice creams. Tomatoes, garlic and herbs grow in abundance in the south and help give southern dishes their characteristic flavours.

Italians take great pleasure in shopping for and cooking with top quality ingredients and the main meal of the day is an important family event, where the food is savoured and news and views are exchanged. Luckily for vegans there is now a large range of animal-free Italian ingredients available. These include vegan versions of mozzarella, Parmesan, blue and soft cheeses, pesto and cream. With all the staple foods such as rice, polenta and pasta (egg-free varieties) being vegan, and the Italians' extensive use of fresh fruit and vegetables, there really is a lot of scope for vegans to cook Italian.

Buon appetito!

THE VEGAN ITALIAN STORECUPBOARD

While seasonal vegetables and fruits form the basis of many Italian recipes and meals are planned according to what is available, certain storecupboard ingredients are used regularly and the following will be useful for creating some authentic-tasting Italian dishes.

Arborio rice Grown in the largest rice growing area in Europe - the Po Valley in northern Italy. Arborio is the *essential* rice for making risotto. The plump, short grains absorb more liquid than other types of rice and it has a rich creamy consistency when cooked.

Beans and chick peas Both feature a great deal in Mediterranean cookery and in Italy the most popular types of bean are cannellini and borlotti. The nutty flavour of chick peas combines especially well with green vegetables. Tinned beans are a useful standby, and cooked dried beans and chick peas can be successfully frozen.

Breadcrumbs Used for toppings, stuffings and for coating food to be fried. Dried white breadcrumbs are preferred and these can easily be made by baking slices of bread in a cool oven until crisp, then whizzing them in a food processor or nutmill. Breadcrumbs can be stored in the freezer and used from frozen.

Capers The small green buds of a Mediterranean bush which are usually sold preserved in brine or vinegar. They can be used to add authenticity to many dishes and sauces, or as a garnish.

Cheeses Some very good vegan versions of Parmesan, mozzarella, blue cheese and soft cream cheeses are available in health food shops and some supermarkets.

Cream Italians are very fond of creamy desserts and in some regions a little cream is added to enrich savoury sauces. Soya cream, available from health food shops, is suitable for use in both sweet and savoury dishes.

Dried mushrooms These are usually the porcini or cep variety and highly prized for their rich flavour. Although expensive, they are only used in small quantities so a little goes a long way. They need to be reconstituted in warm water before use.

Flour Most Italian breads and pizza bases are simply made with plain white flour.

Herbs Italians prefer to use fresh herbs in their cooking and not surprisingly all the commonly used herbs are native to the Mediterranean area. Dried herbs may be used instead of fresh in the recipes, but because dried herbs have a stronger taste the amounts required should be halved.

Basil Also known as sweet basil, this is used extensively in dishes containing tomatoes. Basil is also the main ingredient for pesto. The large fragrant leaves can be used whole in green salads.

Bay leaves The aromatic dried leaves of an evergreen tree native to the Mediterranean area. Bay leaves have a very distinct, strong, slightly bitter flavour and are used in casseroles, soups and sauces.

Fennel seed The dried seeds of a plant belonging to the parsley family. Fennel seeds impart an aniseed/liquorice flavour and are used in dishes containing tomatoes.

Marjoram A herb related to the mint family and one which grows wild on poor, uncultivated soil on Italian hillsides. Used sparingly, this tiny-leafed herb has a very distinct, slightly bitter flavour and is used in soups, tomato and vegetable dishes.

Oregano Sometimes referred to as wild marjoram, oregano is another small-leafed herb that has a natural affinity with tomatoes. It is widely used in sauces and soups and is an essential flavouring for pizzas.

Parsley This popular herb is used liberally in savoury dishes and combines well with other herbs. Italians prefer the flat leaf variety. It is also widely used for garnishing.

Rosemary The thin pine-needle type leaves of this strongly flavoured, sweet and fragrant herb should be used sparingly to flavour vegetable dishes, soups and sauces.

Sage Used quite a lot in Italian cuisine, sage has a musty, slightly bitter flavour. It combines very well with onion and aubergine and is also used in soups and sauces.

Lentils Italians are keen on combining lentils with pasta, either by using them to make sauces for pasta or by cooking lentils and pasta together to produce hearty, filling soups. The type of lentils preferred are the green and brown varieties, which do not break up when cooked. These lentils can also be used in salads.

Olive oil An intrinsic ingredient in Italian cuisine. There are countless varieties to choose from, with tastes varying considerably depending on in which part of the country the oil is produced. Oils made from olives grown in the cooler nothern regions are mild-flavoured, whereas those made from olives grown in the hotter southern climate where they ripen more quickly have a much stronger flavour. Extra-virgin oil is considered to be the best and is also the most expensive. With so many oils to choose from it's a good idea to experiment with small bottles until you find the one that appeals to you most.

Olives Used for both garnishing and as an ingredient, green and black olives are available preserved in oil or brine. Olive paste can also be obtained and this has a very rich, salty flavour.

Pasta Although most pasta is simply made from durum wheat and water some varieties contain egg, so always read the packet. Some shapes have spinach and tomato powder added for colour and flavour. Pasta is naturally high in protein and low in fat and it makes an excellent storecupboard ingredient as it has a very long shelf life.

Pesto A delicious, rich green sauce that originated in Genoa, it is made from fresh basil, pine kernels, olive oil and Parmesan. Pesto can be stirred into plain cooked pasta or added to tomato dishes or soups. A vegan version is available from health food shops and it can also easily be made at home - see under 'Sauces'.

Pine kernels These tiny fragrant nuts are the seeds of a pine tree which is native to the Mediterranean area. Pine kernels have a sweet creamy taste that goes well in sweet and savoury dishes. They can also be used for garnishing and their flavour is enhanced even more if they are slightly toasted before using.

Polenta Made from maizemeal, polenta is a speciality and staple food of northern Italy. It is available in various millings ranging from very coarse to finely ground. There are many ways of serving polenta, from straight-from-the-pot as a thick porridge-type mixture to turned out into a shallow dish, allowed to go cold, cut into shapes and either fried, grilled or baked. Polenta can also be used in biscuit recipes or to thicken soups.

Spices The use of spices in Italian cuisine can be traced back to the days of the Romans. Today, some spices are considered essential for flavouring dishes from particular regions, such as saffron in risotto Milanese and nutmeg in dishes from Bologna, especially those containing spinach. Sweet spices are also used, for flavouring cakes and biscuits.

Cinnamon The dried inner bark of a tree belonging to the laurel family. The highly pungent yet mild sweet flavour makes it a popular spice for adding to cake and biscuit recipes. Cinnamon is available in stick form or ground.

Cloves The name cloves comes from the French word 'clou', meaning 'nail', which is exactly what a whole clove looks like. Cloves are the dried, unopened buds of a tree belonging to the myrtle family and they have a penetrating, sweet, yet pungent flavour. Ground cloves are an essential ingredient in spiced cakes such as panforte.

Nutmeg The aromatic, sweet and spicy seed of an evergreen tree grown mainly in Indonesia and the West Indies. Nutmeg is available either as whole seeds or grated, and special nutmeg graters can be bought to grate the whole seeds. It is used extensively in the Bologna region, especially in dishes containing spinach.

Pepper Probably the world's most popular spice, peppercorns are the dried fruit of a tropical climbing vine. Italians always use black pepper freshly ground in a pepper mill.

Saffron The most expensive of all the spices available, saffron consists of the dried stigmas of a variety of crocus which is native to the Mediterranean area. Bright yellowy/orange in colour, saffron is used very sparingly to impart its colour and pungent, slightly bitter yet aromatic taste to dishes. Saffron strands are usually infused in hot liquid before being added to other ingredients. It is an essential in risotto Milanese.

Vanilla A long slender pod which is the fruit of an orchid native to Central America. A vanilla pod kept in a jar of sugar will impart its delicate flavour to the sugar to be used in cakes and pastries. Pure vanilla extract is also available and can be used sparingly to flavour sweet dishes.

Sun-dried tomatoes These are a relatively new addition to the storecupboard. Sun-dried tomatoes originated in Italy and their taste is intense and unique. They are available dry, for reconstituting in water, or preserved in olive oil, ready to use. A sun-dried tomato paste is also available, which has a more intense, richer flavour than tomato purée.

Tinned tomatoes Italians use tinned 'plum' tomatoes when fresh tomatoes are out of season or expensive. They are available either whole, chopped or crushed and give an authentic flavour to Italian dishes. Sieved crushed tomatoes are called passata.

Tomato purée Used to strengthen the flavour of and add colour to tomato-based dishes. Tomato purée should be used sparingly - too much can give a slightly acidic taste.

Vegetable stock Used in risottos, soups and vegetable and pasta dishes, a good stock is indispensable in the Italian kitchen. It's worth making in bulk and freezing in measured quantities for use as required. Stock can also be kept in the fridge for up to 4 days. To make a good vegetable stock, peel and chop a selection of vegetables such as carrots, courgettes, celery, onions, leeks, potatoes, peppers and the trimmed woody parts from asparagus stems. Put them in a large pan and season with black pepper. Cover with water, bring to the boil and simmer for about 30 minutes, then strain the liquid off through a fine sieve.

Vinegars Balsamic vinegar is a speciality from Modena made from fermented trebbiano grapes, aged in wooden casks for at least 5 years. It has a deep brown colour and a rich spicy sweet flavour. Red and white wine vinegars are also used in salad dressings.

Wine Italy produces more wine than any other country in the world and naturally enough wine is an important feature in Italian cuisine. The climate, soil and landscape all play a significant part in wine production, with each region producing its own unique-tasting wines. Fortified wines such as vermouth are also very popular and these too are used in cooking. Fortunately for vegans many Italian wines and vermouths are available which have been made without the use of any animal products.

Yeast Easy-blend dried yeast is used in all of the recipes requiring yeast. It is simple to use as it does not need to be reconstituted in liquid. The dried yeast is simply mixed with the flour and then made into a dough with warm liquid. Easy-blend yeast is invaluable for making pizza bases and savoury breads and it has a long shelf life.

STARTERS

Italian starters, or antipasti to give them their proper name, are always visu-
ally appealing, consisting of colourful little combinations of vegetables and
salad ingredients - an appetising prelude to the delicious main course to
follow. Many of the starters included here are served cold, which makes them
particularly convenient for serving at dinner parties as they can be prepared
earlier in the day. Plain or savoury-topped crostini are very popular and are
also served as an accompaniment to soups.

Antipasti platter

Choose a selection of the following and arrange them attractively on a serving
platter:

> tomato slices, fennel slices, artichoke hearts, sliced or whole
> mushrooms, black or green olives, pepper slices, chicory
> leaves
>
> **dressing**
>
> 2 tablespoons olive oil
>
> 1 dessertspoon white wine vinegar
>
> 1 teaspoon lemon juice
>
> 1 garlic clove, crushed
>
> 1 dessertspoon finely chopped fresh basil
>
> black pepper

Mix all the dressing ingredients together and spoon over the vegetables on the
platter. Garnish with fresh parsley.

Crostini

> thin slices of bread cut from a French stick
>
> olive oil
>
> vegan 'Parmesan'

Brush the slices of bread with olive oil on both sides. Place under a hot grill until browned on one side, then turn them over and sprinkle with 'Parmesan'. Return to the grill and cook until golden.

To serve crostini with a savoury topping use one of the following instead of the 'Parmesan'.

Mushroom, walnut and olive topping

> 4oz/100g mushrooms, wiped and finely chopped
>
> 1oz/25g walnuts, grated
>
> 1 garlic clove, crushed
>
> 6 black olives, finely chopped
>
> 1 tablespoon olive oil
>
> 1 teaspoon balsamic vinegar
>
> 1 teaspoon dried parsley
>
> black pepper

Heat the oil and gently fry the mushrooms and garlic until soft. Remove from the heat and add the remaining ingredients. Mix thoroughly.

Cannellini, pistachio and olive spread

> 4oz/100g cooked cannellini beans, mashed
>
> 2oz/50g shelled pistachios, ground
>
> 1 tablespoon green olive paste
>
> $1/2$ teaspoon dried marjoram
>
> black pepper

Mix all the ingredients together until well combined.

Marinated peppers *(serves 4)*

12oz/350g yellow peppers

12oz/350g red peppers

1 tablespoon olive oil

2 garlic cloves, crushed

1 tablespoon capers

8 green olives, sliced

black pepper

Grill the peppers until the skin chars and blisters, turning them frequently so that all of the skin blisters. Allow to cool slightly, then peel off the skins and cut the flesh into long strips.

Heat the oil and gently fry the garlic. Remove from the heat and stir in the peppers, capers and olives, season with black pepper and mix thoroughly. Transfer to a serving bowl, cover and chill for a few hours. Serve with thin slices of focaccia (see pages 109/110).

Dressed artichokes *(serves 4)*

12 cooked artichoke hearts, sliced

dressing

1 garlic clove, crushed

3 tablespoons olive oil

1 tablespoon lemon juice

1 dessertspoon balsamic vinegar

1 tablespoon finely chopped fresh parsley

black pepper

Put the sliced artichokes in a bowl, mix the dressing ingredients well and pour over the artichokes. Toss gently, then cover and chill for a couple of hours. Transfer to plates and serve with a salad garnish.

Mushrooms with sun-dried tomatoes *(serves 4)*

1lb/450g mushrooms, wiped and sliced

4 sun-dried tomatoes in oil, drained and finely chopped

2 garlic cloves, crushed

2 tablespoons olive oil

1 dessertspoon sun-dried tomato paste

2 tablespoons finely chopped fresh parsley

black pepper

fresh parsley sprigs

Heat the oil in a large pan and gently fry the garlic. Add the mushrooms, sun-dried tomatoes and paste and chopped parsley, season with black pepper and stir well. Raise the heat and cook whilst stirring for about 3 minutes until the juices begin to run. Serve either hot or cold, garnished with parsley sprigs and accompanied by crostini (see page 20).

Tomato and olive bruschetta *(serves 4)*

4 slices of Italian bread, approx. 1¹/₂ inches/3cm thick

2 garlic cloves, halved

lollo rosso lettuce leaves

fresh basil leaves

8oz/225g tomatoes, chopped

4 sun-dried tomatoes in oil, drained and chopped

2oz/50g mushrooms, wiped and chopped

2oz/50g vegan 'mozzarella', diced

12 black olives, stoned and halved

2 tablespoons olive oil

1 dessertspoon balsamic vinegar

black pepper

1 rounded tablespoon pine kernels, toasted

extra olive oil

Put the tomatoes, mushrooms, olives and 'mozzarella' in a bowl and season with black pepper. Mix the 2 tablespoonfuls of olive oil with the vinegar and add to the tomato mixture. Toss well, cover and leave to marinate for an hour.

Toast both sides of the slices of bread until golden. Rub the bread with the halved garlic cloves. Arrange some lollo rosso and basil leaves on 4 serving plates, put a slice of bread on top and spoon some of the tomato mixture on each slice. Drizzle with some extra olive oil and garnish with the pine kernels.

Walnut and rice balls *(serves 4)*

4oz/100g arborio rice

2oz/50g walnuts, grated

1oz/25g soya flour

1 onion, peeled and finely chopped

1 garlic clove, crushed

1 tablespoon olive oil

1 rounded tablespoon vegan 'Parmesan'

2 fl.oz/50ml white wine

12 fl.oz/350ml vegetable stock

black pepper

$^{1}/_{2}$ teaspoon dried oregano

2oz/50g breadcrumbs

extra olive oil for frying

Heat the tablespoonful of olive oil in a large pan and fry the onion and garlic until softened. Add the rice and oregano and stir around for 1 minute, then the wine and simmer until absorbed. Gradually add the stock, a little at a time, simmering each time until the liquid has been absorbed. Remove from the heat, season with black pepper and add the walnuts, soya flour and 'Parmesan'. Mix thoroughly and refrigerate until cold.

Take rounded dessertspoonfuls of the mixture and form into balls in the palm of the hand, then roll them in the breadcrumbs until completely covered. Fry the balls in hot oil for a few minutes until golden. Drain on kitchen paper and serve with a salad garnish.

Caponata *(serves 4)*

>1lb/450g aubergine, cut into small dice
>
>8oz/225g tin chopped tomatoes
>
>1 onion, peeled and finely chopped
>
>1 celery stick, trimmed and finely sliced
>
>2oz/50g green olives, halved
>
>1 tablespoon capers
>
>2 tablespoons olive oil
>
>1 tablespoon red wine vinegar
>
>1 teaspoon demerara sugar
>
>1 dessertspoon tomato purée
>
>1 dessertspoon finely chopped fresh basil
>
>black pepper
>
>1 tablespoon pine kernels, toasted

Heat the oil in a saucepan and gently fry the onion and celery until soft. Add the aubergine and cook for 10 minutes, stirring frequently. Next add the tomatoes, vinegar, sugar, tomato purée and basil and season with black pepper. Stir well and bring to the boil, cover and simmer gently for about 35 minutes until the vegetables are tender and the mixture is thick, stirring frequently to prevent sticking. Remove from the heat and mix in the olives and capers. Divide between 4 serving bowls, cover and put in the fridge until cold. Garnish with the pine kernels just before serving.

Vegetables in batter *(serves 4)*

1lb/450g mixed prepared vegetables (e.g. whole mushrooms,
  cooked artichoke hearts, courgette slices, cauliflower and
  broccoli florets)

olive oil

lemon wedges

batter

4oz/100g plain flour

4 fl.oz/125ml soya milk

2 tablespoons olive oil

Whisk the soya milk and olive oil with the flour until smooth. Cover and leave
for an hour. Dip the vegetables in the batter, draining off any excess, then deep
fry in olive oil until golden. Drain on kitchen paper and serve immediately
with lemon wedges and a salad garnish.

Fennel, orange and pasta salad *(serves 4)*

6oz/175g fennel bulb, trimmed and finely chopped

2oz/50g tiny pasta shells

1 orange

$1/2$oz/15g walnuts, chopped

1 teaspoon olive oil

$1/4$ teaspoon fennel seeds, crushed

lollo rosso lettuce leaves, shredded

fennel leaves

Blanch the chopped fennel for 1 minute, then rinse under cold running water,
drain and put in a bowl with the walnuts and crushed fennel seeds. Cook the
pasta until tender, rinse with cold water, drain well and add to the bowl. Peel
the orange and remove the pith and membranes. Chop the segments, pour off
the juice and keep this separate, then add the chopped orange to the salad. Mix

the olive oil with 1 tablespoonful of the orange juice and pour over the salad. Toss thoroughly. Arrange some shredded lollo rosso leaves onto 4 serving plates and spoon the salad on top. Garnish with fennel leaves and chill before serving.

SOUPS

The most famous Italian soup must be minestrone, a thick, satisfying mixture of vegetables and tiny pasta shapes that originated in Milan. Minestrone can be made with any combination of vegetables, according to what's in season There are countless variations of this soup and rice is sometimes used instead of pasta. As it is such a filling soup it can be served with focaccia as a light meal rather than a starter.

Other popular Italian soups include those made with lentils and beans. Pesto is often stirred into vegetable soups at the end of cooking and soups are always served in deep rather than shallow bowls, with lashings of 'Parmesan' or 'mozzarella' on top.

Minestrone *(serves 4)*

12oz/350g ripe tomatoes, skinned and chopped

4oz/100g carrot, scraped and diced

4oz/100g leek, trimmed and sliced

4oz/100g courgette, diced

4oz/100g potato, scraped and diced

4oz/100g red cabbage, shredded

2oz/50g small pasta shapes

2 sticks of celery, trimmed and sliced

1 onion, peeled and chopped

2 garlic cloves, crushed

2 tablespoons olive oil

1 rounded tablespoon tomato purée

1 dessertspoon finely chopped fresh parsley

1 dessertspoon finely chopped fresh sage

1 dessertspoon finely chopped fresh basil

2 bay leaves

black pepper

30 fl.oz/900ml vegetable stock

vegan 'Parmesan'

Gently fry all the vegetables for 10 minutes in the oil in a large saucepan. Add the remaining ingredients except the 'Parmesan' and stir well. Bring to the boil, cover and simmer for about 30 minutes until the vegetables are tender and the soup thickens. Stir frequently to prevent sticking. Ladle into serving bowls and sprinkle grated 'Parmesan' on top.

Tomato, red pepper and pesto soup *(serves 4)*

10oz/300g ripe tomatoes, skinned and chopped

8oz/225g red pepper, finely chopped

1 onion, peeled and chopped

1 garlic clove, crushed

1 tablespoon olive oil

1 tablespoon finely chopped fresh parsley

1 tablespoon red pesto

black pepper

20 fl.oz/600ml vegetable stock

vegan 'Parmesan'

Heat the oil in a large saucepan and soften the red pepper, onion and garlic for 5 minutes. Add the tomatoes and fry for a couple of minutes more. Now add the parsley and stock and season with black pepper, stir well and bring to the boil. Cover and simmer gently for about 15 minutes until the vegetables are tender. Allow to cool slightly, then liquidise until smooth. Return to the rinsed pan and stir in the red pesto. Reheat whilst stirring and serve in bowls with grated 'Parmesan'.

Tomato, vegetable and rice soup *(serves 4)*

14oz/400g tin passata

8oz/225g shelled broad beans

4oz/100g courgette, chopped

4oz/100g carrot, scraped and finely chopped

4oz/100g cauliflower, cut into tiny florets

2oz/50g arborio rice

1 onion, peeled and finely chopped

2 garlic cloves, crushed

20 fl.oz/600ml vegetable stock

1 tablespoon olive oil

1 dessertspoon sun-dried tomato paste

1 tablespoon finely chopped fresh basil

1 tablespoon finely chopped fresh parsley

1 bay leaf

black pepper

vegan 'mozzarella', grated

Blanch the broad beans for 2 minutes, drain and rinse under cold water. Slit the skins and remove. Heat the oil in a large saucepan and fry the onion and garlic until softened. Add the rice and fry for 1 minute more, then add the skinned broad beans and the remaining ingredients except the 'mozzarella'. Stir well and bring to the boil, cover and simmer gently for about 20 minutes until the vegetables and rice are tender. Ladle into serving bowls and garnish each bowl with grated 'mozzarella' to serve.

Tuscan bean and celery soup *(serves 4)*

1lb/450g cooked cannellini beans

8oz/225g celery, trimmed and sliced

1 onion, peeled and chopped

1 tablespoon olive oil

30 fl.oz/900ml vegetable stock

2 tablespoons finely chopped fresh parsley

1 bay leaf

black pepper

to finish

2 garlic cloves, crushed

2 tablespoons olive oil

Heat the tablespoonful of olive oil in a large saucepan and gently fry the celery and onion for 10 minutes. Add half of the beans and the vegetable stock, parsley and bay leaf. Season with black pepper and stir well. Bring to the boil, cover and simmer for 15 minutes. Allow to cool slightly, then remove the bay leaf and blend the soup until smooth. Return to the rinsed pan and add the remaining beans. Reheat, whilst stirring, over a low heat. Fry the garlic in the 2 tablespoonfuls of olive oil and stir into the soup just before serving.

Borlotti bean and lentil soup *(serves 4)*

8oz/225g cooked borlotti beans

6oz/175g leek, trimmed and sliced

6oz/175g carrot, scraped and chopped

4oz/100g brown lentils

4oz/100g tomato, skinned and chopped

2 garlic cloves, crushed

26 fl.oz/775ml vegetable stock

1 tablespoon olive oil

1 tablespoon finely chopped fresh sage

1 tablespoon finely chopped fresh oregano

1 bay leaf

black pepper

vegan 'mozzarella', grated

Soak the lentils overnight. Heat the oil in a large saucepan and fry the leek and garlic until soft. Add the drained lentils and stir around for 1 minute. Now add the stock, tomato, carrot, sage, oregano and bay leaf and season with black pepper. Stir well and bring to the boil. Cover and simmer for 30 minutes, stirring occasionally. Allow to cool slightly, then blend half of the soup. Stir into the rest of the soup in the pan, together with the borlotti beans. Bring back to the boil and simmer for 10 minutes. Serve each bowl of soup topped with grated 'mozzarella'.

Chunky courgette, cannellini and pasta soup (serves 4)

8oz/225g courgette

4oz/100g cooked cannellini beans

4oz/100g tomatoes, skinned and chopped

2oz/50g tiny pasta shapes

1 celery stick, trimmed and finely sliced

1 onion, peeled and finely chopped

1 garlic clove, crushed

20 fl.oz/600ml vegetable stock

1 tablespoon olive oil

1 dessertspoon finely chopped fresh rosemary

1 dessertspoon finely chopped fresh parsley

black pepper

vegan 'mozzarella', grated

Gently fry the celery, onion and garlic in the oil in a large saucepan until softened. Quarter the courgette lengthwise and cut each piece into diagonal chunks. Add to the pan together with the remaining ingredients apart from the 'mozzarella'. Stir well and bring to the boil, cover and simmer for 25 minutes until the vegetables and pasta are tender, stirring occasionally to prevent sticking. Ladle into bowls and top with grated 'mozzarella'.

Chestnut soup *(serves 4)*

8oz/225g cooked shelled chestnuts, chopped

1 onion, peeled and chopped

1 celery stick, trimmed and sliced

1 tablespoon olive oil

24 fl.oz/725ml vegetable stock

2 tablespoons fortified wine

black pepper

Heat the oil in a large saucepan and gently fry the onion and celery until soft. Add the chestnuts and fry for 2 minutes more, then the remaining ingredients and stir well. Bring to the boil, cover and simmer for 15 minutes until tender. Remove from the heat and allow to cool slightly. Blend the soup until smooth, then return to the rinsed pan and reheat whilst stirring.

SAUCES

Sauces are an essential part of Italian cuisine and are used extensively in all regions. Unlike sauces from other cultures, Italian sauces are easy to prepare and rely on the freshness of the ingredients used to give good results, rather than on lengthy and complicated cooking techniques.

With such an abundance of tomatoes grown in Italy it is hardly surprising that tomato-based sauces are among the most popular. Really ripe tomatoes need to be used in recipes requiring fresh tomatoes.

Fresh tomato sauce

1lb/450g ripe tomatoes, skinned and chopped

1 dessertspoon olive oil

2 garlic cloves, crushed

1 dessertspoon tomato purée

1 rounded dessertspoon finely chopped fresh basil

Heat the oil in a saucepan and gently fry the garlic. Add the remaining ingredients and stir well. Bring to the boil and simmer gently until the tomatoes become pulpy and the sauce thickens.

Fresh tomato and onion sauce

As for fresh tomato sauce, but use 1 tablespoonful of olive oil and fry a finely chopped onion with the garlic before adding the remaining ingredients.

Raw tomato sauce

1lb/450g ripe tomatoes, skinned and finely chopped

1 shallot, peeled and grated

1 garlic clove, crushed

1 tablespoon finely chopped fresh basil

2 tablespoons olive oil

1 dessertspoon white wine vinegar

Mix all the ingredients well and chill before serving.

Creamy tomato sauce

A rich sauce that is very good with gnocchi (see page 91).

1lb/450g ripe tomatoes, skinned and chopped

1 onion, peeled and chopped

2 garlic cloves, crushed

1 tablespoon olive oil

2 fl.oz/50ml white wine

2 fl.oz/50ml vegetable stock

1 tablespoon finely chopped fresh oregano

1 tablespoon finely chopped fresh basil

black pepper

4 tablespoons vegan 'cream'

Heat the oil and fry the onion and garlic until soft. Add the remaining ingredients except the cream and stir well. Bring to the boil, cover and simmer for 15 minutes. Allow to cool, then blend until smooth. Add the 'cream' and reheat to serve.

Tinned tomato sauce

14oz/400g tin chopped tomatoes

1 onion, peeled and finely chopped

1 celery stick, trimmed and finely chopped

1 garlic clove, crushed

1 tablespoon olive oil

1 dessertspoon finely chopped fresh oregano

1 teaspoon tomato purée

black pepper

Heat the oil and gently fry the onion, celery and garlic until softened. Add the remaining ingredients and bring to the boil. Cover and simmer, stirring occasionally, for 20 minutes.

Bolognese sauce

Probably best known for being served with spaghetti, Bolognese sauce goes just as well with tagliatelle or other pasta. It can also be used in lasagne.

14oz/400g tin crushed tomatoes

6oz/175g carrot, scraped

4oz/100g minced natural textured vegetable protein

2oz/50g button mushrooms, wiped and sliced

2 celery sticks, trimmed and finely sliced

1 onion, peeled and finely chopped

4 fl.oz/125ml white wine

10 fl.oz/300ml vegetable stock

1 tablespoon tomato purée

1 tablespoon olive oil

1 tablespoon finely chopped fresh oregano

1/4 teaspoon grated nutmeg

black pepper

2 tablespoons soya milk or vegan 'cream' (optional)

Heat the oil in a large saucepan and fry the onion and celery until soft. Grate half the carrots and finely chop the rest. Add to the pan together with the remaining ingredients except the soya milk or 'cream'. Stir well and bring to the boil, cover and simmer for 30-35 minutes until the mixture thickens. Stir in the soya milk or 'cream' just before serving if required.

Besciamella

A classic white sauce that is poured over cannelloni or other baked pasta dishes.

> 1¹/₂oz/40g vegan margarine
> 1¹/₂oz/40g plain flour
> 20 fl.oz/600ml hot soya milk
> black pepper
> grated nutmeg or bay leaf (optional)

If a bay leaf is used this should be added to the soya milk when heating, then discarded.

Melt the margarine in a saucepan. When it starts to bubble, gradually add the flour, stirring all the time. Cook for 1 minute whilst stirring, then remove from the heat. Stir in the soya milk a little at a time until fully combined. Season with black pepper and add the nutmeg if using. Return to the heat and simmer whilst stirring for 10 minutes until the sauce has thickened.

Vegan 'cheese' sauce

Add 2oz/50g grated vegan 'cheese' to the besciamella sauce before seasoning.

Herb sauce

Add 2 tablespoons finely chopped fresh herbs of your choice to the besciamella sauce after all the milk has been stirred in.

Walnut sauce

There are many variations of this unusual, rich sauce, some containing finely chopped fresh parsley. It can be used as a topping for crostini or as a stuffing for mushrooms. Alternatively it may be thinned with more soya milk and combined with tagliatelle.

> 2oz/50g walnuts, grated
>
> 1oz/25g breadcrumbs
>
> 1 garlic clove, crushed
>
> 4 tablespoons soya milk
>
> 2 tablespoons olive oil
>
> 1 tablespoon lemon juice
>
> black pepper

Mix all the ingredients together until well combined.

Mushroom and wine sauce

This sauce is excellent with plain cooked vegetables such as potatoes, cauliflower or broccoli.

> 8oz/225g mushrooms, wiped and finely chopped
>
> 1 small onion, peeled and finely chopped
>
> 1 garlic clove, crushed
>
> 2 tablespoons olive oil
>
> 2 tablespoons finely chopped fresh parsley
>
> 1/2oz/15g plain flour

black pepper

2 fl.oz/50ml white wine

4 fl.oz/125ml vegetable stock

Heat the oil and fry the onion and garlic until soft. Add the mushrooms and parsley and fry until the juices begin to run, then add the flour and mix thoroughly. Gradually add the wine and then the stock, stirring all the time. Season with black pepper and slowly bring to the boil. Continue stirring until the sauce thickens.

Salsa verde

This easily-made piquant sauce can be used as a dressing for salads or cooked vegetables. When thinned with a little of the cooking water, it is also good for flavouring plain pasta.

2oz/50g fresh parsley

1 tablespoon capers

1 garlic clove

2 tablespoons lemon juice

3 tablespoons olive oil

black pepper

Put all the ingredients in a blender and blend until smooth.

Pesto

A classic Genoese sauce with an unmistakeable flavour. Used in small quantities, pesto is added to soups and tomato-based dishes to enrich the flavours. It is also used in the same way as salsa verde to flavour plain pasta.

> 2oz/50g fresh basil leaves
>
> 1oz/25g pine kernels
>
> 1 garlic clove
>
> black pepper
>
> 4 tablespoons olive oil
>
> 2 tablespoons vegan 'Parmesan'

Put the garlic, pine kernels and 'Parmesan' in a food processor and chop finely, then add the basil leaves. Finally pour in the olive oil, season with black pepper and blend until smooth.

Parsley and walnut pesto

Replace the basil in the pesto recipe with 2oz/50g fresh parsley and the pine kernels with 1oz/25g walnuts.

Red pesto

Add 1 tablespoonful of sun-dried tomato paste and 8oz/225g red pepper that has been roasted, skinned and chopped to the ingredients for pesto.

Gremolata

Not really a sauce, more of a garnish that I like to use for soups and risottos.

> 3 tablespoons finely chopped fresh parsley
>
> 1 garlic clove, crushed
>
> 1 tablespoon finely grated lemon peel

Mix until well combined.

RISOTTO

Countries all over the world have their own speciality rice recipes and Italy is no exception, with its classic risotto dishes. Risotto is unlike any other rice dish because it is made with arborio rice, grown in the Po Valley in northern Italy. Arborio is short-grained, plumpish rice, which absorbs more liquid than other types to give a rich, creamy texture when cooked. The liquid is added a little as a time and the rice is stirred frequently during cooking. A selection of risotto recipes is given below, but once the technique of cooking risotto has been mastered almost any vegetables or beans can be added to make your own variations.

Risotto Milanese *(serves 4)*

8oz/225g arborio rice

1 onion, peeled and finely chopped

1 tablespoon olive oil

black pepper

4 fl.oz/125ml white wine

24 fl.oz/725ml hot vegetable stock

$^1/_2$ teaspoon saffron strands

$^1/_2$oz/15g vegan margarine (optional)

1 tablespoon vegan 'Parmesan'

Heat the oil in a large heavy-based saucepan and gently fry the onion until softened. Add the rice and fry for another minute. Stir in the wine and simmer gently until absorbed, then add the stock a little at a time, making sure the liquid is absorbed before adding more. Dissolve the saffron in the last bit of stock and continue simmering until it has all been taken up, stirring frequently during the cooking to prevent sticking. Season with black pepper and stir in the margarine (if using) and 'Parmesan'. Transfer to a warmed serving dish.

Pea and mushroom risotto *(serves 4)*

8oz/225g arborio rice

8oz/225g shelled peas

4oz/100g button mushrooms, wiped and sliced

1 onion, peeled and finely chopped

2 garlic cloves, crushed

1 tablespoon olive oil

$1/2$ teaspoon saffron strands

1 bay leaf

1 tablespoon finely chopped fresh parsley

black pepper

4 fl.oz/125ml white wine

24 fl.oz/725ml hot vegetable stock

$1/2$oz/15g vegan margarine (optional)

1 tablespoon vegan 'Parmesan'

Follow the instructions for risotto Milanese but fry the garlic with the onion, add the mushrooms with the rice, and add the peas, parsley and bay leaf after the wine.

Courgette and spinach risotto *(serves 4)*

8oz/225g arborio rice

8oz/225g courgette, halved lengthwise and sliced

6oz/175g frozen cooked chopped spinach, thawed

1 onion, peeled and finely chopped

1 tablespoon olive oil

$^1/_4$ teaspoon grated nutmeg

black pepper

1 bay leaf

4 fl.oz/125ml white wine

24 fl.oz/725ml hot vegetable stock

$^1/_2$oz/15g vegan margarine (optional)

1 tablespoon vegan 'Parmesan'

Follow the instructions for risotto Milanese but stir in the courgette, spinach, nutmeg and bay leaf after adding the wine and note that no saffron is used.

Cauliflower, parsley and walnut risotto *(serves 4)*

8oz/225g arborio rice

12oz/350g cauliflower, cut into tiny florets

3oz/75g fresh parsley, finely chopped

1 onion, peeled and finely chopped

2 garlic cloves, crushed

1 tablespoon olive oil

1 bay leaf

black pepper

4 fl.oz/125ml white wine

24 fl.oz/725ml hot vegetable stock

1oz/25g walnuts, finely chopped

$^1/_2$oz/15g vegan margarine (optional)

1 tablespoon vegan 'Parmesan'

Following the instructions for risotto Milanese, fry the garlic with the onion, add the cauliflower, bay leaf and parsley after the wine, omit the saffron, and stir in the walnuts once the risotto is cooked.

Mixed bean risotto *(serves 4)*

8oz/225g arborio rice

8oz/225g green beans, topped and tailed and cut into small
diagonal chunks

4oz/100g broad beans, skinned

4oz/100g cooked borlotti beans

1 onion, peeled and finely chopped

2 garlic cloves, crushed

1 tablespoon olive oil

1 bay leaf

black pepper

1 dessertspoon finely chopped fresh marjoram

4 fl.oz/125ml white wine

24 fl.oz/725ml hot vegetable stock

$1/2$oz/15g vegan margarine (optional)

1 tablespoon vegan 'Parmesan'

Follow the risotto Milanese recipe, but fry the garlic with the onion and add the mixed beans, bay leaf and marjoram after the wine. No saffron is used.

MAIN COURSES

A traditional Italian meal always consists of at least two courses: a starter and a main course with a salad or a vegetable dish. Dishes suitable to serve as main courses can also be found in the Stuffed Vegetables, Pasta and Pizza sections.

Broccoli- and spinach-stuffed pancakes *(serves 4)*

pancakes

3oz/75g plain flour

1oz/25g soya flour

5 fl.oz/150ml soya milk

5 fl.oz/150ml water

1 tablespoon olive oil

vegan margarine

filling

8oz/225g broccoli, finely chopped

8oz/225g cooked chopped spinach

2oz/50g fennel, finely chopped

1 onion, peeled and finely chopped

1 garlic clove, crushed

1 tablespoon olive oil

4 fl.oz/125ml vegetable stock

black pepper

1 teaspoon finely chopped fresh marjoram

pinch of grated nutmeg

6 fl.oz/175ml soya milk

1 rounded dessertspoon cornflour

1oz/25g vegan 'mozzarella', grated

vegan margarine

vegan 'Parmesan'

Make the pancake mixture by combining the plain and soya flour and adding the olive oil, soya milk and water. Whisk until smooth, cover and leave for 2 hours.

Gently fry the onion, garlic and fennel in the oil until softened. Add the broccoli and vegetable stock and bring to the boil. Cover and simmer for about 10 minutes, stirring occasionally, until the broccoli is just tender. Take off the stove. Dissolve the cornflour in the soya milk and add to the pan together with the spinach, marjoram and nutmeg. Season with black pepper and mix thoroughly. Return to the heat and bring to the boil whilst stirring. Continue stirring until the mixture thickens. Remove from the heat and stir in the 'mozzarella'.

Heat a little vegan margarine in a 7 inch/18cm diameter non-stick frying pan until really hot. Pour in 2 tablespoonfuls of batter and swirl around until the base of the pan is covered. Cook for a minute or two until golden underneath, loosen the edges with a knife, carefully turn over and cook the underside until browned. Repeat with the remaining batter to make 8 pancakes.

Divide the vegetable mixture between the pancakes and roll each one up to enclose the filling. Place the pancakes with the joins underneath in a lightly-oiled baking dish. Spread the top of each pancake with a little vegan margarine and sprinkle with grated 'Parmesan'. Bake in a preheated oven at 180°C/350°F/Gas mark 4 for 25 minutes.

Savoury nut balls with tomato and pepper sauce (*serves 4*)

nut balls
3oz/75g hazelnuts, ground

3oz/75g breadcrumbs

3oz/75g natural, minced, textured vegetable protein

1 onion, peeled and finely chopped

2 garlic cloves, crushed

1 tablespoon olive oil

8 fl.oz/225ml vegetable stock

1 rounded teaspoon dried parsley

1 teaspoon dried sage

black pepper

1 rounded tablespoon hazelnut butter

1/2oz/15g soya flour

3 tablespoons water

extra olive oil

sauce

12oz/350g ripe tomatoes, skinned and chopped

12oz/350g mixed peppers, finely chopped

1 garlic clove, crushed

1 tablespoon olive oil

1 dessertspoon tomato purée

1 teaspoon dried oregano

black pepper

garnish

chopped fresh parsley

Soak the textured vegetable protein in the vegetable stock for 30 minutes. Heat the tablespoonful of olive oil in a large pan and fry the onion and garlic until soft. Remove from the heat and stir in the ground hazelnuts and breadcrumbs. Add the soaked textured vegetable protein, parsley and sage and season with black pepper. Stir well. Mix the soya flour with the hazelnut butter and water and add. Mix thoroughly until the ingredients bind together. Take rounded dessertspoonfuls of the mixture and roll into balls in the palm of the hand. Put these on a plate, cover and refrigerate for a few hours, then brush the nut balls all over with olive oil and bake in a preheated oven at 180°C/350°F/Gas mark 4 for 25 minutes.

Heat the oil for the sauce and gently soften the chopped peppers and garlic. Add the remaining sauce ingredients and stir well. Raise the heat, cover and simmer for 10 minutes until the tomatoes are pulpy and the sauce thickens. Pour the sauce over the nut balls and garnish with chopped fresh parsley to serve.

Courgette and tomato gratin *(serves 4)*

1¹/₂lb/675g courgettes, thinly sliced

12oz/350g ripe tomatoes, skinned and chopped

4 garlic cloves, crushed

2 shallots, peeled and sliced

2 tablespoons olive oil

3 tablespoons fortified wine

1 dessertspoon sun-dried tomato paste

black pepper

1 tablespoon finely chopped fresh oregano

1 bay leaf

topping

1oz/25g breadcrumbs

1oz/25g vegan 'mozzarella', grated

1 tablespoon vegan 'Parmesan'

1 rounded teaspoon dried parsley

Heat the oil in a saucepan and soften the garlic and shallot. Add the courgettes, tomatoes, wine, tomato paste, oregano and bay leaf and season with black pepper. Raise the heat and simmer gently for 5 minutes whilst stirring. Transfer to a shallow lightly-oiled baking dish.

Mix the topping ingredients together and sprinkle over the vegetables. Bake in a preheated oven at 180°C/350°F/Gas mark 4 for 25 minutes until golden.

Asparagus, mushroom and walnut gratin (*serves 4*)

2lb/900g asparagus, trimmed

8oz/225g button mushrooms, wiped and sliced

2 garlic cloves, crushed

1 tablespoon olive oil

1oz/25g plain flour

2 rounded tablespoons finely chopped fresh parsley

black pepper

20 fl.oz/600ml soya milk

topping

2oz/50g breadcrumbs

1oz/25g walnuts, finely chopped

2 tablespoons vegan 'Parmesan'

1 rounded dessertspoon vegan margarine

Cut the asparagus into 1 inch/2.5cm lengths and steam until just tender. Heat the oil in a large saucepan and fry the mushrooms and garlic until the juices begin to run. Add the flour and mix until well combined, then gradually stir in the soya milk. Add the parsley and season with black pepper. Bring to the boil whilst stirring and continue stirring until the sauce thickens. Add the asparagus and transfer to a shallow lightly-oiled baking dish.

Melt the margarine over a low heat and stir in the breadcrumbs. Remove from the heat and add the walnuts and 'Parmesan'. Spoon the mixture evenly over the vegetables and bake in a preheated oven at 180°C/350°F/Gas mark 4 for 20-25 minutes until golden brown.

Herby rice loaf wrapped in spinach *(serves 4)*

This loaf can also be served cold. After removing it from the tin allow it to cool slightly, then cover it and put it in the fridge for several hours or overnight until cold.

1lb/450g fresh tender spinach leaves

loaf

8oz/225g arborio rice

2oz/50g carrot, scraped and grated

2oz/50g red pepper, finely chopped

2oz/50g green pepper, finely chopped

2oz/50g vegan 'mozzarella', grated

2oz/50g mushrooms, wiped and finely chopped

1 onion, peeled and finely chopped

2 garlic cloves, crushed

1 rounded tablespoon vegan 'Parmesan'

1 rounded tablespoon finely chopped fresh parsley

1 rounded tablespoon finely chopped fresh oregano

1 rounded tablespoon finely chopped fresh marjoram

1 tablespoon olive oil

black pepper

24 fl.oz/725ml vegetable stock

Gently fry the onion and garlic in the oil in a large saucepan until softened. Add the rice and fry for 1 minute whilst stirring. Add the remaining loaf ingredients except the 'mozzarella' and 'Parmesan' and stir well. Bring to the boil, cover and simmer gently until the liquid has been absorbed. Remove from the heat and stir in the 'mozzarella' and 'Parmesan'.

Wash the spinach leaves and remove any thick stalks, then blanch them in boiling water for 30 seconds and drain thoroughly. Line a 10 inch/25cm loaf tin with foil and lightly oil. Use half the spinach leaves to line the tin, making sure there is an overhang to fold over the filling. Build up the layers so that no gaps remain. Spoon half of the loaf mixture into the spinach-lined tin and press down evenly. Take three-quarters of the remaining leaves and spread these evenly over the filling to make a spinach layer. Spoon the rest of the filling on top and press down evenly. Fold the overhanging leaves over the filling and spread the remaining leaves on top. Cover with foil and bake in a preheated oven at 180°C/350°F/Gas mark 4 for 1 hour.

Leave in the tin for 10 minutes, then carefully invert onto a serving plate. Cut into thick slices to serve.

Vegetable and chick pea stew with soft polenta (*serves 4*)

8oz/225g quick-cook polenta

40 fl.oz/1200ml water

stew

12oz/350g ripe tomatoes, skinned and chopped

8oz/225g cooked chick peas

8oz/225g courgette, sliced

4oz/100g red pepper, sliced

4oz/100g green pepper, sliced

4oz/100g yellow pepper, sliced

2oz/50g button mushrooms, wiped and sliced

1 red onion, peeled and chopped

1 celery stick, trimmed and sliced

2 garlic cloves, crushed

4 sun-dried tomatoes in oil, drained and chopped

4 fl.oz/125ml red wine

3 fl.oz/75ml vegetable stock

1 tablespoon olive oil

1 dessertspoon tomato purée

2 bay leaves

black pepper

1 dessertspoon finely chopped fresh oregano

1 dessertspoon finely chopped fresh basil

topping

vegan 'Parmesan'

chopped walnuts

Heat the oil in a large pan and fry the onion, celery and garlic until soft. Add the tomatoes and cook until pulpy, then the remaining stew ingredients except the chick peas. Stir well, bring to the boil, cover and simmer for 20 minutes, stirring frequently. Add the chick peas and continue simmering for another 10 minutes.

Meanwhile, make the polenta. Put the water in a large pan and bring to the boil. Gradually add the polenta, whisking all the time to prevent lumps forming. Simmer for 5-10 minutes whilst stirring, until the mixture thickens.

Serve the stew on a bed of polenta and sprinkle with 'Parmesan' and chopped walnuts.

Broccoli and mushroom Florentine *(serves 4)*

1^1/$_2$lb/675g broccoli, chopped

12oz/350g frozen cooked chopped spinach, thawed

8oz/225g button mushrooms, wiped and halved

1 onion, peeled and finely chopped

12 fl.oz/350ml vegetable stock

18 fl.oz/550ml soya milk

1oz/25g cornflour

1 tablespoon olive oil

1 dessertspoon finely chopped fresh marjoram

1 dessertspoon finely chopped fresh parsley

^{1}/$_2$ teaspoon grated nutmeg

black pepper

topping

1oz/25g breadcrumbs

1oz/25g vegan 'mozzarella', grated

1 rounded teaspoon dried parsley

Fry the onion in the oil in a large saucepan until soft. Add the broccoli, vegetable stock, marjoram, parsley and nutmeg and season with black pepper. Stir well and bring to the boil, cover and simmer gently until the broccoli is just tender. Dissolve the cornflour in the soya milk and add to the pan together with the spinach and mushrooms. Bring to the boil whilst stirring and continue stirring for a minute or two until the sauce thickens. Transfer to a shallow lightly-oiled baking dish.

Mix the topping ingredients together and spoon evenly over the vegetables. Bake in a preheated oven at 180°C/350°F/Gas mark 4 for about 25 minutes until golden brown.

Aubergine and lentil layered pie *(serves 4)*

1lb/450g aubergine, thinly sliced

14oz/400g tin passata

6oz/175g brown lentils

1 onion, peeled and finely chopped

2 garlic cloves, crushed

1 dessertspoon olive oil

2 tablespoons fortified wine

2 tablespoons water

1 tablespoon sun-dried tomato paste

1 tablespoon finely chopped fresh basil

1 dessertspoon finely chopped fresh marjoram

1 bay leaf

black pepper

extra olive oil

sauce

³/₄oz/20g vegan margarine

³/₄oz/20g plain flour

10 fl.oz/300ml hot soya milk

black pepper

1oz/25g vegan 'mozzarella', grated

topping

vegan 'Parmesan'

finely chopped fresh parsley

Soak the lentils in water for a couple of hours, then drain and rinse. Put them into a pan of fresh water and bring to the boil, cover and simmer for about 30 minutes until tender. Drain and set aside.

Heat the dessertspoonful of olive oil and gently fry the onion and garlic until softened. Remove from the heat and add the drained lentils, passata, wine, water, tomato paste, marjoram, basil and bay leaf. Season with black pepper and stir well. Brush the aubergine slices on both sides with olive oil and grill until golden. Spoon half of the lentil mixture into a shallow lightly-oiled baking dish, arrange half the aubergine slices on top and repeat these layers.

Melt the margarine in a small pan and when it starts to bubble stir in the flour. Cook gently for 1 minute. Remove from the heat and gradually add the soya milk, stirring briskly so that no lumps form. Add the 'mozzarella' and season with black pepper. Return to the heat, bring to the boil whilst stirring and continue stirring until the sauce thickens. Pour the sauce over the aubergine slices and sprinkle with grated 'Parmesan'. Cover with foil and bake in a preheated oven at 180°C/350°F/Gas mark 4 for 1 hour. Sprinkle the top with finely chopped fresh parsley before serving.

Fennel, borlotti bean and polenta bake *(serves 4)*

base

12oz/350g fennel bulb, trimmed and sliced

8oz/225g cooked borlotti beans

4oz/100g button mushrooms, wiped and sliced

1 onion, peeled and chopped

2 garlic cloves, crushed

14oz/400g tin crushed tomatoes

2 tablespoons olive oil

1 dessertspoon tomato purée

1 dessertspoon pesto

2 bay leaves

$1/2$ teaspoon fennel seeds

black pepper

2 fl.oz/50ml vegetable stock

topping

6oz/175g polenta

1 rounded teaspoon dried sage

1 rounded teaspoon dried parsley

1 rounded tablespoon vegan 'Parmesan'

30 fl.oz/900ml water

First cook the polenta. Put the water in a large saucepan and bring to the boil. Mix the sage, parsley and 'Parmesan' with the dry polenta and gradually add to the boiling water, whisking all the time to prevent lumps. Lower the heat and simmer, whilst stirring frequently, for 10-15 minutes until the mixture thickens. Spoon the polenta into a lined baking dish (flattening it with a wet spoon so that it is about $3/4$ inch/2cm thick). Cover and put in the fridge until cold.

Heat the oil in a large pan and gently fry the fennel, onion and garlic for 10 minutes. Add the remaining base ingredients and stir well. Transfer the mixture to a shallow lightly-oiled baking dish. Cut the cold polenta into small triangles and arrange these on top of the vegetables. Bake in a preheated oven at 180°C/350°F/Gas mark 4 for 30-35 minutes until golden.

STUFFED VEGETABLES

Italians have a fondness for baked stuffed vegetables and serve them either as a starter or as a main course. Although specific recipes for fillings are given here, in Italy they sometimes simply fill vegetables with leftovers such as risotto or whatever other savoury mixture is to hand. The first three recipes here, for stuffed artichokes, mushrooms and tomatoes, are all suitable as starters, while the remaining recipes can be served with accompaniments as main courses.

Artichokes with mushroom and hazelnut filling *(serves 4 as starter)*

4 globe artichokes, trimmed

lemon juice

filling

2oz/50g mushrooms, wiped and finely chopped

1oz/25g hazelnuts, grated and toasted

1/2oz/15g breadcrumbs

1 garlic clove, crushed

1 tablespoon olive oil

1 tablespoon white wine

1 teaspoon dried parsley

black pepper

dressing

2 tablespoons olive oil

1 tablespoon lemon juice

black pepper

Brush the trimmed artichoke surfaces with lemon juice, then put them in a pan of boiling water and cook for 35-40 minutes until tender. Drain well, cut away the inner leaves and remove the chokes.

Heat the oil for the filling and gently fry the mushrooms and garlic until the juices begin to run. Remove from the heat and add the remaining filling ingredients, mix thoroughly and fill each artichoke with some of this mixture. Put the artichokes in a baking dish. Whisk the olive oil and lemon juice together and season with black pepper. Spoon over the stuffed artichokes. Bake in a preheated oven at 180°C/350°F/Gas mark 4 for 10 minutes.

Nutty garlic-stuffed mushrooms
(serves 4 as starter)

16 medium-sized cup mushrooms

olive oil

filling

1oz/25g breadcrumbs

1oz/25g ground almonds

1oz/25g walnuts, grated

1oz/25g vegan 'mozzarella', grated

2 large garlic cloves, crushed

2 tablespoons fortified wine

1 dessertspoon olive oil

1 rounded teaspoon dried parsley

black pepper

Wipe the mushrooms and remove the stalks, then brush the outsides with olive oil and place them upside down in an oiled baking dish. Chop the stalks and fry these with the garlic for a couple of minutes in the dessertspoonful of olive oil. Remove from the heat and add the remaining filling ingredients. Mix thoroughly until everything binds together.

Spoon some of the mixture into each mushroom cap, pressing it down firmly and evenly. Bake in a preheated oven at 180°C/350°F/Gas mark 4 for 15-20 minutes until the mushrooms are just tender.

Mushroom-, 'mozzarella'- and walnut-stuffed tomatoes *(serves 4 as starter)*

2 large tomatoes (each approx. 12oz/350g)

filling

3oz/75g mushrooms, wiped and finely chopped

2oz/50g breadcrumbs

1oz/25g vegan 'mozzarella', grated

1oz/25g walnuts, finely chopped

2 garlic cloves, crushed

1 dessertspoon olive oil

1 tablespoon finely chopped fresh parsley

black pepper

vegan 'Parmesan'

Cut the tomatoes in half in a zig-zag pattern. Carefully remove the insides and chop finely. Put the chopped inners into a sieve and drain off as much liquid as possible. Dry the inside of the tomato shells with kitchen paper and put them in a lightly-oiled baking dish.

Heat the oil and gently fry the mushrooms and garlic for 2 minutes. Add the chopped tomato inners and cook for a further minute. Remove from the heat and mix in the remaining filling ingredients except the 'Parmesan' until everything binds together. Carefully fill each of the tomato shells with some of the mixture. Sprinkle the tops with 'Parmesan' and bake in a preheated oven at 180°C/350°F/Gas mark 4 for 10-15 minutes until just cooked.

Stuffed courgettes with tomato and oregano sauce (*serves 4*)

4 courgettes (each approx. 8oz/225g)

filling

4oz/100g mushrooms, wiped and finely chopped

1 onion, peeled and finely chopped

2 garlic cloves, crushed

1 tablespoon olive oil

1oz/25g pine kernels, grated

1 rounded tablespoon finely chopped fresh parsley

black pepper

sauce

8oz/225g tomatoes, skinned and chopped

1 teaspoon olive oil

1 garlic clove, crushed

1 tablespoon fresh chopped oregano

black pepper

topping

1/2oz/15g pine kernels

Cut the courgettes in half lengthwise and scoop out the flesh, leaving the shell about 1/4 inch/5mm thick. Cut each courgette half in two crosswise to make 16 hollowed-out boat shapes.

Heat the oil for the filling in a saucepan and gently fry the onion and garlic until softened. Chop the scooped-out courgette flesh finely and add to the pan together with the mushrooms and parsley. Season with black pepper and cook whilst stirring for 2 minutes. Remove from the heat and stir in the grated pine kernels, then carefully fill the courgette shells with the mixture and arrange the filled shells in a lightly-oiled baking dish.

Heat the oil for the sauce and fry the garlic. Add the remaining sauce ingredients and stir well. Bring to the boil, then simmer until the tomatoes become pulpy and the sauce thickens. Spoon the sauce over the filled courgettes and sprinkle the pine kernels on top. Cover with foil and bake in a preheated oven at 180°C/350°F/Gas mark 4 for about 30 minutes until just done.

Stuffed baked peppers *(serves 4)*

4 peppers (each approx. 6oz/175g)

vegan 'Parmesan'

fresh chopped parsley

filling

6oz/175g courgette, finely chopped

4oz/100g arborio rice

1 onion, peeled and finely chopped

1 garlic clove, crushed

1 dessertspoon olive oil

1 dessertspoon finely chopped fresh oregano

1 bay leaf

black pepper

10 fl.oz/300ml vegetable stock

1oz/25g walnuts, finely chopped

sauce

8oz/225g tomatoes, skinned and chopped

1 dessertspoon olive oil

1 garlic clove, crushed

1 teaspoon tomato purée

1 tablespoon water

Cut each pepper in half lengthwise and remove the stalks, membranes and seeds. Blanch the pepper halves in boiling water for 2 minutes, drain and place in an oiled baking dish.

Heat the oil for the filling in a saucepan and fry the onion and garlic until softened. Add the rice and fry for 1 minute more. Add the remaining filling ingredients except the walnuts and stir well. Bring to the boil, cover and simmer gently until the liquid has been absorbed. Remove from the heat and stir in the walnuts. Fill the pepper halves with the rice mixture.

Gently fry the garlic for the sauce in the oil in a small pan. Add the remaining sauce ingredients and stir well. Simmer until the tomatoes become pulpy and the mixture thickens. Spoon the sauce over the filled peppers and sprinkle with grated 'Parmesan'. Cover with foil and bake in a preheated oven at 180°C/350°F/Gas mark 4 for 30 minutes. Garnish with fresh chopped parsley when serving.

Savoury stuffed onions (*serves 4*)

> 4 large onions
>
> **filling**
>
> 1oz/25g natural minced textured vegetable protein
>
> 2oz/50g mushrooms, wiped and finely chopped
>
> 2 garlic cloves, crushed
>
> 4 fl.oz/125ml vegetable stock
>
> 1 tablespoon olive oil
>
> 1 dessertspoon sun-dried tomato paste
>
> 1 dessertspoon finely chopped fresh sage
>
> 1 dessertspoon finely chopped fresh parsley
>
> black pepper

Soak the textured vegetable protein for 30 minutes in the stock. Put the onions, with skins on, in a large pan and cover with water. Bring to the boil and simmer for 5 minutes. Drain them and leave to cool. Peel the onions, then carefully remove the centre of each one, leaving a 'shell' of about 3 or 4 layers thick. Put the 'shells' in an oiled baking dish. Finely chop the removed onion and fry in the oil with the garlic and mushrooms until soft. Add the vegetable protein and any remaining stock together with all other filling ingredients. Raise the heat and simmer for 3 minutes. Divide the filling between the onion 'shells', pressing down firmly after each spoonful. Cover with foil and bake in a preheated oven at 180°C/350°F/Gas mark 4 for about 40 minutes until tender.

Aubergines with mushroom and walnut filling (*serves 4*)

2 aubergines (each approx. 10oz/300g)

filling

4oz/100g mushrooms, wiped and finely chopped

4oz/100g breadcrumbs

2oz/50g walnuts, grated

1 onion, peeled and finely chopped

2 garlic cloves, crushed

2 tablespoons olive oil

extra olive oil

1 dessertspoon sun-dried tomato paste

1 dessertspoon finely chopped fresh oregano

black pepper

chopped pine kernels

Cut the aubergines in half lengthwise and scoop out the flesh, leaving shells of about ¼ inch/5mm thick. Brush these inside and out with olive oil and place in an oiled baking dish.

Finely chop the aubergine flesh and fry with the onion and garlic in the 2 tablespoonfuls of oil for 10 minutes, stirring frequently. Add the mushrooms and fry for a further minute. Remove from the heat and add the breadcrumbs, walnuts, tomato paste and oregano. Season with black pepper and mix thoroughly. Spoon the filling into the aubergine shells and sprinkle the tops with chopped pine kernels. Cover with foil and bake in a preheated oven at 180°C/350°F/Gas mark 4 for 45 minutes until cooked. Remove the foil and bake for 5 minutes more to brown.

Savoury rice-filled cabbage leaves with tomato sauce (*serves 4*)

16 savoy cabbage leaves

filling

4oz/100g arborio rice

4oz/100g red pepper, finely chopped

4oz/100g yellow pepper, finely chopped

2oz/50g mushrooms, wiped and finely chopped

1 onion, peeled and finely chopped

1 garlic clove, crushed

1 tablespoon olive oil

14 fl.oz/400ml vegetable stock

1 dessertspoon finely chopped fresh sage

black pepper

1oz/25g walnuts, finely chopped

1oz/25g vegan 'mozzarella', grated

sauce

tinned tomato sauce (see page 35)

chopped pine kernels

Gently fry the red and yellow pepper, onion and garlic for 5 minutes in the oil. Add the mushrooms and rice and stir around for 1 minute. Mix in the sage and stock and season with black pepper. Bring to the boil, cover and simmer gently until the liquid has been absorbed. Remove from the heat and stir in the walnuts and 'mozzarella'.

Blanch the cabbage leaves in boiling water for 3 minutes, then drain well and cut out the hard stalk at the base of each leaf. Divide the filling between the leaves and fold them around the filling to make little parcels. Put the parcels with the joins underneath in a lightly-oiled shallow baking dish. Spoon the tomato sauce over the top and sprinkle with chopped pine kernels. Cover with foil and bake in a preheated oven at 180°C/350°F/Gas mark 4 for 30 minutes.

PIZZA

Now known throughout the world as the ultimate fast food, pizzas originated in Naples as an inexpensive and filling savoury snack. They are baked in traditional open brick ovens there and sold in pizzerias and bakeries and from street market stalls. Although almost any ingredient can be made into a pizza topping, the original Neapolitan pizza had only a frugal topping of tomatoes and cheese.

Pizzas make ideal party foods and the ingredients can easily be doubled to make large oblong pizzas, suitable for cutting into slices or little squares.

Pizza dough

8oz/225g plain flour

1 teaspoon easy-blend yeast

$^1/_2$ teaspoon salt

1 tablespoon olive oil

approx. 4 fl.oz/125ml warm water

Mix the flour, yeast and salt in a bowl. Add the olive oil and then gradually the water until a soft dough forms. Turn out onto a floured board and knead well. Return to the bowl, cover with a piece of oiled cling film and leave in a warm place for 1 hour until risen. Knead the dough again before rolling out or shaping.

Mushroom and olive pizza (serves 4)

1 quantity of pizza dough

topping

6oz/175g tomatoes, skinned and finely chopped

4oz/100g button mushrooms, wiped and sliced

1 onion, peeled and finely chopped

2 garlic cloves, crushed

1 dessertspoon olive oil

1 teaspoon olive oil

1 teaspoon tomato purée

black pepper

1 rounded dessertspoon finely chopped fresh oregano

6 black olives, stoned, rinsed and halved

1oz/25g vegan 'mozzarella', grated

extra olive oil

Roll or stretch the dough into a 10 inch/25cm diameter circle. Put on an oiled baking sheet and leave in a warm place for 30 minutes to rise.

Heat the dessertspoonful of olive oil and gently fry the onion and garlic until soft. Add the chopped tomato and fry until it is just beginning to soften. Remove from the heat and stir in the tomato purée and oregano, season with black pepper and set aside. Fry the mushrooms in the teaspoonful of oil in a small pan until the juices begin to run.

Brush the pizza base lightly with olive oil and spread the tomato mixture evenly over it. Arrange the mushrooms and olives on top and bake in a preheated oven at 200°C/400°F/Gas mark 6 for 10 minutes. Remove from the oven and sprinkle the 'mozzarella' evenly on top. Return to the oven for a further 5 minutes until golden brown.

Sun-dried tomato and sweetcorn pizzas *(makes 4)*

1 quantity of pizza dough

topping

6oz/175g sweetcorn kernels

6oz/175g tomatoes, skinned and chopped

2oz/50g sun-dried tomatoes in oil, drained and finely chopped

1 onion, peeled and finely chopped

1 garlic clove, crushed

1 dessertspoon olive oil

1 teaspoon sun-dried tomato paste

1 dessertspoon finely chopped fresh oregano

black pepper

vegan 'Parmesan'

dried parsley

extra olive oil

Divide the dough into 4 equal pieces and roll or shape each piece into a 5¹⁄₂ inch/14cm diameter round. Put them on an oiled baking sheet and leave in a warm place for 30 minutes to rise.

Heat the dessertspoonful of olive oil and gently fry the onion and garlic until soft. Add the fresh tomatoes, sun-dried tomatoes, tomato paste and oregano. Season with black pepper and stir well. Raise the heat and simmer until the tomatoes are pulpy and the mixture thickens. Remove from the heat and stir in the sweetcorn kernels.

Brush the pizza bases lightly with olive oil and divide the topping between them. Spread it out evenly and sprinkle with 'Parmesan' and dried parsley. Bake in a preheated oven at 200°C/400°F/Gas mark 6 for 12–15 minutes until golden.

Roasted pepper and caper pizzettes *(makes 8)*

1 quantity of pizza dough

topping

6oz/175g tomatoes, skinned and chopped

4oz/100g red pepper

4oz/100g yellow pepper

1 shallot, peeled and finely chopped

1 garlic clove, crushed

1 dessertspoon olive oil

1 teaspoon sun-dried tomato paste

1 rounded dessertspoon finely chopped fresh oregano

1 tablespoon capers

black pepper

vegan 'Parmesan'

extra olive oil

Divide the dough into 8 equal pieces and roll or shape each piece into a small oval, about ¼ inch/5mm thick. Put them on an oiled baking sheet and leave in a warm place for 30 minutes to rise.

Cook the peppers under a hot grill until the skins start to brown and bubble, turning them until they are browned all over. Allow to cool slightly, then peel off the skins and finely chop the pepper flesh. Heat the dessertspoonful of oil and fry the shallot and garlic until softened. Add the tomatoes, tomato paste and oregano and season with black pepper. Cook until the tomatoes are pulpy and the sauce thickens. Remove from the heat and add the chopped peppers and the capers. Mix well.

Brush the bases lightly with olive oil and divide the topping between them. Spread it out evenly and sprinkle with 'Parmesan'. Bake in a preheated oven at 200°C/400°F/Gas mark 6 for about 12 minutes until browned.

Pizza calzone (*serves 4*)

1 quantity of pizza dough

filling

6oz/175g mixed peppers, finely chopped

4oz/100g tomatoes, skinned and chopped

2oz/50g mushrooms, wiped and chopped

1oz/25g vegan 'mozzarella', grated

1 onion, peeled and finely chopped

1 garlic clove, crushed

1 tablespoon olive oil

1 teaspoon sun-dried tomato paste

1 dessertspoon finely chopped fresh oregano

black pepper

extra olive oil

Divide the dough into 4 equal pieces and roll or shape them into a 7 inch/18cm diameter circle. Leave in a warm place for 30 minutes to rise.

Heat the tablespoonful of olive oil and gently fry the peppers, onion and garlic for 5 minutes. Add the tomatoes, mushrooms, tomato paste and oregano and season with black pepper. Cook for 2 minutes more. Remove from the heat and stir in the 'mozzarella'. Mix well, then divide the mixture between the 4 pastry circles, spooning it onto one half of each circle only. Dampen the edges with water and fold the dough over to enclose the filling, pressing the edges together to join. Transfer them to an oiled baking sheet and make 3 small slits in the top of each one. Brush with olive oil and bake in a preheated oven at 180°C/350°F/Gas mark 4 for about 20 minutes until golden brown.

PASTA

Italians have reputedly been eating pasta for well over 700 years. Legend has it that Marco Polo introduced it to Italy on his return from China, where he had found noodles a popular dish. However, many Italians dispute this and believe that a form of pasta has been made since the days of the Romans.

Today, pasta is eaten in most parts of Italy, but it is probably more popular in the south of the country, with each region having its own favourite types and distinctive ways of serving it. Pasta is an economical and very nutritious food, high in protein and carbohydrates and low in fat. All varieties are incredibly easy to cook, but read packet instructions for length of cooking time, as this varies between shapes. The Italians like their pasta cooked al dente, which means that it is slightly resistant when bitten and not too soft.

There are literally dozens of pasta shapes available and as it is such a versatile food it can easily be combined with a few simple ingredients to make a substantial main course for a dinner party, or a quick and nourishing supper dish for one.

Tagliatelle with garlic and parsley dressing (*serves 4*)

8oz/225g tagliatelle

2 large garlic cloves, crushed

4 rounded tablespoons finely chopped fresh parsley

3 tablespoons olive oil

Cook the tagliatelle until al dente. Meanwhile, heat the oil in a large pan and gently fry the garlic and parsley for a couple of minutes. Drain the tagliatelle and add. Remove from the heat, toss thoroughly and serve immediately.

Spaghetti with fried courgettes *(serves 4)*

1lb/450g small courgettes, thinly sliced
8oz/225g spaghetti
2 tablespoons olive oil
vegan 'Parmesan'
black pepper

Heat the oil and fry the courgettes until just tender. Meanwhile, bring a large pan of water to the boil, add the spaghetti and cook until al dente. Drain the spaghetti and transfer it to a large warmed serving bowl. Add the courgettes and season with black pepper. Toss until well combined. Garnish with 'Parmesan' to serve.

Asparagus, mushroom and walnut fusilli *(serves 4)*

8oz/225g fusilli or spirals
1lb/450g asparagus, trimmed and cut into 1/2 inch/1cm lengths
6oz/175g mushrooms, wiped and finely chopped
1 onion, peeled and finely chopped
2 garlic cloves, crushed
2 dessertspoons olive oil
8 fl.oz/225ml vegetable stock
10 fl.oz/300ml soya milk
2 rounded tablespoons finely chopped fresh parsley
black pepper
2 rounded dessertspoons cornflour

2oz/50g walnuts, chopped

grated vegan 'blue cheese'

Fry the mushrooms and garlic in 1 dessertspoonful of oil in a small pan until the juices begin to run and the mushrooms soften. Remove from the heat and blend with the soya milk in a blender.

Heat the other dessertspoonful of oil in a large pan and gently fry the onion until softened. Add the asparagus, vegetable stock and parsley and season with black pepper, stir well and bring to the boil. Cover and simmer for about 10 minutes until the asparagus is tender. Meanwhile, cook the pasta in a pan of boiling water until al dente.

Mix the cornflour with the mushroom purée until smooth and add this to the asparagus. Stir well, bring to the boil whilst stirring and continue stirring until the sauce thickens. Drain the fusilli, add to the sauce and toss. Pour into a warmed serving dish and garnish with the walnuts and grated 'blue cheese'.

Mushroom, lentil and olive tagliatelle *(serves 4)*

8oz/225g tagliatelle verdi

12oz/350g button mushrooms, wiped and halved

8oz/225g brown lentils

4oz/100g tomatoes, skinned and chopped

1 onion, peeled and finely chopped

2 celery sticks, trimmed and finely chopped

2 garlic cloves, crushed

1 tablespoon olive oil

4 fl.oz/125ml white wine

1 rounded tablespoon black olive paste

1 tablespoon finely chopped fresh parsley

black pepper

12 black olives, halved

Cook the lentils until tender, then drain and set aside. Gently fry the onion, celery and garlic in the oil in a large pan until softened. Add the mushroons and fry for 2 minutes whilst stirring. Now add the lentils, tomatoes, wine, olive paste and parsley and stir well. Season with black pepper and bring to the boil. Cover and simmer for 10 minutes, stirring frequently. Meanwhile, cook the tagliatelle until al dente. Drain and serve with the sauce. Garnish with the black olive halves.

Linguine with avocado, mushroom and walnut sauce *(serves 4)*

8oz/225g linguine

1 large or 2 small avocado pears, peeled, stoned and mashed

10oz/300g button mushrooms, wiped and sliced

2oz/50g walnuts, chopped

1 onion, peeled and finely chopped

1 tablespoon olive oil

8 fl.oz/225ml soya milk

1/2oz/15g cornflour

1 rounded tablespoon vegan 'cream cheese'

1 tablespoon finely chopped fresh parsley

black pepper

Heat the oil in a large pan and gently fry the onion until soft, then add the mushrooms and fry for 2 minutes more. Dissolve the cornflour in the soya milk and add to the pan together with the mashed avocado, 'cream cheese' and parsley. Season with black pepper and stir well. Bring to the boil slowly whilst stirring and continue to stir for a minute or two until the sauce thickens. Keep warm.

Cook the linguine until al dente, drain and add to the sauce together with half the chopped walnuts. Toss well, then transfer to a serving dish or plates and garnish with the remaining walnuts.

Conchiglie with pepper, courgette and chick pea sauce *(serves 4)*

8oz/225g conchiglie

1lb/450g mixed peppers

1lb/450g courgette, sliced

8oz/225g cooked chick peas

3 tablespoons olive oil

1 onion, peeled and finely chopped

2 garlic cloves, crushed

4 fl.oz/125ml vegetable stock

1 dessertspoon finely chopped fresh oregano

black pepper

chopped fresh parsley

Place the peppers under a hot grill and cook until the skins start to brown and bubble. turning them until browned all over. Allow to cool, then peel off the skins and finely chop the flesh.

Heat 1 tablespoonful of oil and gently fry the garlic and chopped peppers for 5 minutes. Put in a blender with the vegetable stock and blend until smooth. Fry the onion in the remaining oil until softened, then add the courgettes and oregano and season with black pepper. Fry for about 10 minutes until the courgettes are just tender, stirring occasionally. Add the pepper sauce and the chick peas and simmer gently for 10 minutes whilst stirring frequently.

Meanwhile, cook the pasta until al dente, then drain and add to the sauce. Stir well to combine. Transfer to a serving bowl or plates and garnish with chopped fresh parsley.

Creamy broccoli and spinach lasagne *(serves 4)*

8 sheets lasagne

filling

1lb/450g broccoli, finely chopped

8oz/225g frozen cooked chopped spinach, thawed

1 onion, peeled and finely chopped

2oz/50g vegan 'mozzarella', grated

2 rounded tablespoons vegan 'cream cheese'

1 tablespoon olive oil

6 fl.oz/175ml vegetable stock

20 fl.oz/600ml soya milk

$^1/_2$oz/15g cornflour

1 dessertspoon finely chopped fresh marjoram

$^1/_4$ teaspoon grated nutmeg

black pepper

topping

2oz/50g breadcrumbs

1oz/25g walnuts, finely chopped

2 tablespoons vegan 'Parmesan'

1 rounded dessertspoon vegan margarine

1 dessertspoon dried parsley

Heat the oil in a saucepan and fry the onion until soft. Add the broccoli and vegetable stock and bring to the boil, cover and simmer gently until the broccoli is just cooked. Dissolve the cornflour in the soya milk and add to the pan together with the remaining filling ingredients. Stir well and again bring to the boil. Continue stirring until the sauce thickens slightly.

Spoon $^1/_3$rd of the mixture into a 12 x 8 inch/30 x 20cm lasagne dish and top with 4 sheets of lasagne. Repeat these layers and finish with the remaining filling.

Melt the margarine over a low heat, then stir in the breadcrumbs. Remove from the heat and add the other topping ingredients. Mix well and spread the topping evenly over the filling. Cover with foil and bake in a preheated oven at 180°C/350°F/Gas mark 4 for 30 minutes, then remove the foil and bake for a further 5-10 minutes until golden brown.

Lasagne verdi *(serves 4)*

8 sheets lasagne verdi

filling

1lb/450g courgette, thinly sliced

8oz/225g green lentils

14oz/400g tin crushed tomatoes

2oz/50g fennel bulb, finely chopped

1 onion, peeled and finely chopped

2 garlic cloves, crushed

4 fl.oz/125ml white wine

4 fl.oz/125ml vegetable stock

1 tablespoon tomato purée

2 tablespoons olive oil

1 rounded tablespoon finely chopped fresh oregano

1 rounded tablespoon finely chopped fresh basil

1 teaspoon fennel seed

1 bay leaf

black pepper

topping

4oz/100g frozen cooked chopped spinach, thawed

10 fl.oz/300ml soya milk

$^1/_2$oz/15g cornflour

pinch of grated nutmeg

2oz/50g breadcrumbs

2 rounded tablespoons vegan 'Parmesan'

1 dessertspoon dried parsley

Cook the lentils until tender, drain and set aside. Gently fry the onion, garlic and chopped fennel in the oil in a large pan until softened. Add the lentils and the remaining filling ingredients and stir well. Bring to the boil, cover and simmer for 10 minutes.

Spoon 1/3rd of the filling into a 12 x 8 inch/30 x 20cm lasagne dish and cover with 4 sheets of lasagne. Repeat these layers and finish with a layer of filling.

Dissolve the cornflour in the milk, pour into a saucepan and add the spinach and nutmeg. Bring to the boil whilst stirring and continue stirring until the sauce thickens. Pour the sauce over the filling. Mix the breadcrumbs with the 'Parmesan' and parsley and sprinkle evenly over the sauce. Cover with foil and bake in a preheated oven at 180°C/350°F/Gas mark 4 for 30 minutes. Remove the foil and bake for a further 5-10 minutes until golden on top.

Pasta and vegetable Romana *(serves 4)*

8oz/225g courgette, thinly sliced

4oz/100g mushrooms, wiped and sliced

4oz/100g pasta spirals

2oz/50g red pepper, sliced

2oz/50g green pepper, sliced

1 stick of celery, trimmed and finely sliced

1 onion, peeled and chopped

2 garlic cloves, crushed

14oz/400g tin crushed tomatoes

3 fl.oz/75ml vegetable stock

3 fl.oz/75ml white wine

1 tablespoon olive oil

1 dessertspoon capers

1 dessertspoon finely chopped fresh oregano

1 dessertspoon finely chopped fresh basil

1 bay leaf

black pepper

topping

6oz/175g vegan 'cream cheese'

3 fl.oz/75ml soya milk

2oz/50g breadcrumbs

1oz/25g hazelnuts, chopped

2 tablespoons vegan 'Parmesan'

1 rounded teaspoon dried parsley

Cook the pasta until al dente, drain and set aside. Heat the oil in a large pan and gently fry the onion, celery and garlic until soft. Stir in the crushed tomatoes, wine and vegetable stock, then add the rest of the vegetables together with the capers, oregano, basil and bay leaf. Season with black pepper and stir well. Bring to the boil, cover and simmer for 5 minutes. Remove from the heat and add the pasta. Mix well and spoon into a shallow baking dish.

Mix the 'cream cheese' with the soya milk and spread evenly over the vegetables and pasta. Mix the breadcrumbs with the hazelnuts, 'Parmesan' and parsley and sprinkle on top. Cover the dish with foil and bake in a preheated oven at 180°C/350°F/Gas mark 4 for 30 minutes, then remove the foil and bake for 5-10 minutes more until browned.

Cauliflower and macaroni Florentine (*serves 4*)

1lb/450g cauliflower, cut into small florets

14oz/400g tin crushed tomatoes

8oz/225g frozen cooked chopped spinach, thawed

4oz/100g wholewheat macaroni

2oz/50g vegan 'mozzarella', grated

1 onion, peeled and finely chopped

2 garlic cloves, crushed

1 tablespoon olive oil

1 tablespoon tomato purée

1 dessertspoon finely chopped fresh marjoram

pinch of grated nutmeg

black pepper

4 fl.oz/125ml vegetable stock

topping

2oz/50g breadcrumbs

2 rounded tablespoons vegan 'Parmesan'

1 dessertspoon dried parsley

Heat the oil and fry the onion and garlic until softened. Add the cauliflower and vegetable stock and bring to the boil. Cover and simmer gently until the cauliflower is just tender. Remove from the heat and add the crushed tomatoes, spinach, 'mozzarella', tomato purée, marjoram and nutmeg. Cook the macaroni until al dente, drain and add to the mixture. Season with black pepper and mix thoroughly. Transfer to a shallow baking dish.

Mix the topping ingredients and spread evenly over the top. Cover with foil and bake in a preheated oven at 180°C/350°F/Gas mark 4 for 30 minutes. Remove the foil and bake for a further 5-10 minutes until golden brown.

Creste di gallo with creamy tomato and asparagus sauce (*serves 4*)

8oz/225g creste di gallo

1lb 2oz/500g tomatoes, skinned and chopped

1lb 2oz/500g asparagus, trimmed

1 onion, peeled and chopped

2 garlic cloves, crushed

1 tablespoon olive oil

2 fl.oz/50ml white wine

6 fl.oz/175ml vegetable stock

1 tablespoon finely chopped fresh oregano

1 dessertspoon finely chopped fresh basil

black pepper

4 tablespoons vegan 'cream'

topping

2oz/50g breadcrumbs

1¹/₂oz/40g pine kernels, chopped

2 tablespoons vegan 'Parmesan'

1 dessertspoon dried parsley

Fry the onion and garlic in the oil until soft. Add the tomatoes, wine, stock, oregano and basil and season with black pepper. Stir well and bring to the boil, then cover and simmer for 10 minutes. Allow to cool slightly and blend until smooth.

Cut the asparagus into 1 inch/2.5cm lengths and steam until just tender. Add to the sauce together with the cream and stir until well combined.

Cook the creste di gallo until al dente, drain and add to the sauce. Pour into a shallow baking dish. Mix the topping ingredients and spoon evenly over the top. Cover with foil and bake in a preheated oven at 180°C/350°F/Gas mark 4 for 25 minutes, then remove the foil and bake for 5 minutes more until golden.

Spinach and pistachio cannelloni (*serves 4*)

16 cannelloni tubes

filling

1lb/450g fresh spinach leaves

6oz/175g vegan 'cream cheese'

2oz/50g shelled pistachios, grated

1 onion, peeled and finely chopped

1 dessertspoon olive oil

1 dessertspoon finely chopped fresh marjoram

pinch of grated nutmeg

black pepper

sauce

1oz/25g vegan margarine

1oz/25g plain flour

20 fl.oz/600ml soya milk

black pepper

2oz/50g vegan 'blue cheese', grated

1 tablespoon finely chopped fresh parsley

topping

1oz/25g breadcrumbs

1oz/25g shelled pistachios, finely chopped

Wash the spinach leaves and put them into a large pan with only the water that clings to them. Cover and cook gently until tender. Drain and allow to cool, then squeeze out as much water as possible. Chop the spinach finely. Heat the oil in a saucepan and gently fry the onion until soft. Remove from the heat and add the chopped spinach and remaining filling ingredients, mixing thoroughly. Fill each of the cannelloni tubes with some of this mixture and put them in an oiled baking dish.

Melt the margarine and when it begins to bubble add the flour. Stir until well combined, then cook for 1 minute whilst stirring. Remove from the heat and add the soya milk a little at a time, mixing each addition in until smooth. Stir in the grated 'cheese' and parsley and season with black pepper. Return to the heat and bring to the boil. Simmer whilst stirring for 10 minutes. Pour the sauce evenly over the cannelloni, making sure that it runs between each tube and covers the tops completely.

Mix the breadcrumbs with the pistachios and sprinkle over the sauce. Cover with foil and bake in a preheated oven at 180°C/350°F/Gas mark 4 for 30 minutes. Remove the foil and bake for a further 5-10 minutes until browned.

Aubergine and hazelnut cannelloni *(serves 4)*

16 cannelloni tubes

filling

1lb/450g aubergine, finely chopped

2oz/50g hazelnuts, grated

1 onion, peeled and finely chopped

2 garlic cloves, crushed

2 tablespoons olive oil

1 rounded tablespoon vegan 'cream cheese'

1 tablespoon finely chopped fresh parsley

black pepper

sauce

14oz/400g tin crushed tomatoes

4oz/100g tomatoes, skinned and chopped

1 dessertspoon olive oil

1 garlic clove, crushed

1 dessertspoon finely chopped fresh basil

1 dessertspoon sun-dried tomato paste

black pepper

topping

1oz/25g breadcrumbs

1oz/25g hazelnuts, flaked

Fry the aubergine, onion and garlic for 20 minutes in the 2 tablespoons olive oil until soft. Stir frequently to prevent sticking. Remove from the heat and add the remaining filling ingredients. Mix well, then fill each of the cannelloni tubes with some of the mixture and put them in an oiled baking dish.

Heat the oil for the sauce and gently fry the garlic. Add the other sauce ingredients and stir well, then raise the heat and simmer for 5 minutes. Pour the sauce evenly over the cannelloni, making sure that it runs between each tube and covers the tops completely.

Mix the breadcrumbs with the hazelnuts and sprinkle over the sauce. Cover with foil and bake in a preheated oven at 180°C/350°F/Gas mark 4 for 30 minutes, then remove the foil and bake for a further 5-10 minutes until golden.

VEGETABLES

As well as serving little vegetable dishes as starters, an Italian main course invariably includes a separate vegetable dish and it is for this purpose that the recipes in this section are intended. Vegetables such as broccoli, cauliflower, courgette, mushrooms, broad beans, fennel, green beans, peas and asparagus are also frequently served with just a simple dressing of olive oil and lemon juice.

Spinach with chick peas *(serves 4)*

1lb/450g spinach

8oz/225g cooked chick peas

2 tablespoons olive oil

1 garlic clove, crushed

1 tablespoon finely chopped fresh parsley

black pepper

toasted pine kernels

Wash the spinach carefully and put it into a pan with only the water that clings to the leaves. Cook gently until tender, drain and press out excess water, and chop roughly. Heat the oil and fry the garlic. Add the spinach, chick peas and parsley and season with black pepper. Toss, then cook gently until heated through. Transfer to a warmed serving dish and garnish with toasted pine kernels.

Baked fennel with garlic crumbs *(serves 4)*

1lb/450g fennel bulb, trimmed

1 tablespoon olive oil

1 dessertspoon olive oil

1/2oz/15g breadcrumbs

1 large garlic clove, crushed

black pepper

lemon juice

vegan 'Parmesan'

Cut the fennel into even-sized slices and put them in a pan of water to which a squeeze of lemon juice has been added. Bring to the boil, simmer for 10 minutes and drain. Heat the tablespoonful of oil and gently fry the fennel for 3 minutes. Transfer to a baking dish and season with black pepper. Fry the garlic in the dessertspoonful of oil in a small pan, add the breadcrumbs and stir around for 1 minute. Sprinkle the breadcrumbs over the fennel and bake in a preheated oven at 180°C/350°F/Gas mark 4 for 10-15 minutes until golden. Sprinkle with grated 'Parmesan' to serve.

Peperonata *(serves 4)*

1lb/450g mixed peppers, sliced

12oz/350g ripe tomatoes, skinned and chopped

1 onion, peeled and chopped

2 garlic cloves, crushed

2 tablespoons olive oil

1 teaspoon tomato purée

1 dessertspoon chopped fresh oregano

2 bay leaves

black pepper

chopped fresh parsley

Heat the oil in a large pan and gently fry the pepper, onion and garlic for 10 minutes. Add the remaining ingredients apart from the parsley and simmer uncovered, stirring frequently, until the mixture is thick and the peppers are tender, adding a little water if necessary to prevent sticking. Garnish with chopped fresh parsley.

Aubergine and tomato pie *(serves 4)*

1lb/450g aubergine

olive oil

tinned tomato sauce (see page 35)

2oz/50g vegan 'mozzarella', grated

2 tablespoons vegan 'Parmesan'

Cut the aubergine into long slices of about 1/4 inch/5mm thick. Brush both sides with olive oil and put them under a hot grill for a few minutes each side until golden. Place alternate layers of aubergine, tomato sauce and 'mozzarella' in a lightly-oiled baking dish. Sprinkle the 'Parmesan' on top and bake in a preheated oven at 180°C/350°F/Gas mark 4 for 35-40 minutes until golden brown.

Broccoli with garlic and lemon dressing *(serves 4)*

1lb/450g broccoli, cut into florets

1 tablespoon olive oil

2 garlic cloves, crushed

2 tablespoons lemon juice

black pepper

Steam the broccoli until just tender while making the dressing. Heat the oil in a saucepan and gently fry the garlic, then add the lemon juice and season with black pepper. Carefully stir in the broccoli. Transfer to a warmed serving dish.

Sweet and sour onions *(serves 4/6)*

1lb/450g pickling onions

2 tablespoons olive oil

2 tablespoons white wine vinegar

1 tablespoon demerara sugar

4 cloves

1 bay leaf

Peel the onions and boil them for 5 minutes. Put the other ingredients in a pan and heat gently until the sugar dissolves. Add the drained onions and cook for 15 minutes until tender. Stir frequently so that the onions are completely coated. Serve either hot or cold.

Baked garlic and rosemary potatoes *(serves 4)*

2lb/900g potatoes

2 tablespoons olive oil

2 garlic cloves, sliced

1 dessertspoon chopped fresh rosemary

Scrub the potatoes and cut in half lengthwise. Cut each half into 1 inch/2.5cm thick slices. Heat the oil in a large pan and add the potatoes. Fry for 10 minutes, turning occasionally. Stir in the garlic and rosemary and transfer to a shallow baking dish. Bake in a preheated oven at 180°C/350°F/Gas mark 4 for about 30 minutes until golden.

Parsley potatoes *(serves 4)*

2lb/900g potatoes, peeled and sliced ¹/₄ inch/5mm thick

4 tablespoons finely chopped fresh parsley

7 fl.oz/200ml soya milk

black pepper

fresh parsley sprigs

Put the potatoes, chopped parsley and soya milk in a large saucepan and season with black pepper. Bring to the boil and simmer gently for 10 minutes, stirring occasionally. Transfer to a baking dish, cover tightly with foil and bake in a preheated oven at 190°C/375°F/Gas mark 5 for 30 minutes until done. Garnish with parsley sprigs and serve.

Potato and tomato bake *(serves 6)*

2lb/900g potatoes, scraped and diced

8oz/225g ripe tomatoes, skinned and chopped

4oz/100g red pepper, finely sliced

2oz/50g button mushrooms, wiped and sliced

1 onion, peeled and finely chopped

2 garlic cloves, crushed

1 tablespoon capers

2 tablespoons olive oil

4 tablespoons water

1 dessertspoon sun-dried tomato paste

1 dessertspoon finely chopped fresh oregano

black pepper

vegan 'Parmesan'

chopped fresh parsley

Heat the oil and fry the onion, red pepper and garlic until soft. Add the mushrooms and fry for a further minute. Dissolve the tomato paste in the water and add, together with the tomatoes and oregano. Season with black pepper and stir well. Bring to the boil, cover and simmer gently until the tomatoes are pulpy and the mixture thickens.

Meanwhile, boil the potatoes until just done. Drain them and add to the sauce together with the capers. Mix well, then spoon into a lightly-oiled baking dish and sprinkle with 'Parmesan'. Cover with foil and bake in a preheated oven at 180°C/350°F/Gas mark 4 for 30 minutes. Garnish with chopped parsley to serve.

Potato croquettes *(serves 4)*

2lb/900g potatoes, peeled

1^{1}/$_{2}$oz/40g breadcrumbs

1oz/25g vegan margarine

1 tablespoon vegan 'Parmesan'

1 dessertspoon dried parsley

black pepper

olive oil

Cut the potatoes into even-sized chunks and boil until cooked. Drain them and dry off over a low heat, then mash with the margarine. Stir in the 'Parmesan' and parsley and season with black pepper. Cover and keep in the fridge until cold. Take rounded tablespoonfuls of the mashed potato and shape into croquettes. Roll each croquette in breadcrumbs until completely covered. Put them on an oiled baking tray and brush them with olive oil. Bake in a preheated oven at 180°C/350°F/Gas mark 4 for 30 minutes until golden brown.

Potato, spinach and 'mozzarella' croquettes *(serves 4)*

Follow the recipe for potato croquettes but omit the 'Parmesan' and add the following to the mashed potato:

4oz/100g frozen cooked chopped spinach, thawed and pressed in a sieve to remove excess liquid

2oz/50g vegan 'mozzarella', grated

Potato gnocchi *(serves 4)*

1lb/450g potatoes, scraped

5oz/150g plain flour

$^1/_2$oz/15g vegan margarine

1 rounded tablespoon vegan 'Parmesan'

1 rounded dessertspoon dried parsley

black pepper

creamy tomato sauce (see page 34)

chopped fresh parsley

Cut the potatoes into even-sized chunks and cook. Drain and dry off over a low heat, then mash with the margarine and stir in the 'Parmesan', parsley and flour. Season with black pepper and mix until a soft doughy mixture forms. Put this dough in the fridge until cold.

Take rounded teaspoonfuls of the mixture and roll into balls in the palm of the hand. Make an indent in the top of each one using a fork. Bring a large pan of water to the boil and drop half of the gnocchi into the boiling water. Cook for about 5 minutes until they rise to the surface. Remove with a slotted spoon and transfer to a lightly-oiled baking dish, then repeat with the remaining gnocchi. Spoon the creamy tomato sauce on top and bake in a preheated oven at 180°C/350°F/Gas mark 4 for 15 minutes. Garnish with chopped parsley and serve.

Potato and spinach gnocchi *(serves 4)*

Follow the recipe for potato gnocchi but omit the 'Parmesan' and add:

4oz/100g frozen cooked chopped spinach, thawed and pressed in a sieve to remove excess liquid

$^1/_4$ teaspoon grated nutmeg

Cannellini beans in tomato sauce *(serves 4)*

30oz/850g tinned cannellini beans, drained and rinsed

14oz/400g tin crushed tomatoes

8oz/225g carrot, scraped and finely chopped

2 celery sticks, trimmed and finely sliced

1 onion, peeled and finely chopped

2 garlic cloves, crushed

1 tablespoon olive oil

1 dessertspoon finely chopped fresh sage

1 dessertspoon finely chopped fresh basil

black pepper

Heat the oil in a large saucepan and gently fry the onion, garlic and celery until softened. Add the remaining ingredients and stir well. Bring to the boil, cover and simmer for about 30 minutes until the vegetables are tender and the mixture thickens. Stir frequently to prevent sticking.

Baked asparagus *(serves 4)*

1lb/450g asparagus, trimmed

4oz/100g tomato, skinned and chopped

1 small onion, peeled and finely chopped

1 garlic clove, crushed

1 tablespoon olive oil

1 tablespoon red wine

1 dessertspoon sun-dried tomato paste

1 dessertspoon finely chopped fresh oregano

black pepper

topping

1oz/25g breadcrumbs

1 tablespoon vegan 'Parmesan'

1 teaspoon dried parsley

1 rounded teaspoon vegan margarine

1 garlic clove, crushed

Heat the margarine for the topping and fry the garlic. Add the remaining topping ingredients, stir around for 1 minute and set aside.

Cut the asparagus stalks in half and steam until just tender. Fry the onion and garlic in the oil until soft. Add the tomato, tomato paste, oregano and red wine and season with black pepper. Cook gently until the tomatoes are pulpy and the sauce thickens.

Arrange the asparagus in a shallow lightly-oiled baking dish. Spoon the sauce along the centre and sprinkle the breadcrumbs on top. Cover with foil and bake in a preheated oven at 180°C/350°F/Gas mark 4 for 10 minutes, then remove the foil and bake for 5-10 minutes more until browned.

Cauliflower in mushroom sauce *(serves 4)*

1lb/450g cauliflower, cut into florets

sauce

6oz/175g button mushrooms, wiped and sliced

1oz/25g dried porcini

1 onion, peeled and finely chopped

2 garlic cloves, crushed

1 tablespoon olive oil

2 tablespoons finely chopped fresh parsley

2 fl.oz/50ml white wine

1oz/25g plain flour

black pepper

soya milk

extra parsley

Put the dried porcini in a bowl and cover with warm water. Leave to soak for 20 minutes, then drain them into a bowl and rinse them in clean water. Dry on kitchen paper and chop them finely. Strain the soaking liquid into a measuring jug and make up to 12 fl.oz/350ml with soya milk.

Heat the oil in a saucepan and fry the onion and garlic until soft. Add the porcini, button mushrooms and 2 tablespoons parsley and fry for a few minutes until the juices begin to run. Stir in the flour and wine and cook gently until well combined. Season with black pepper and gradually add the soya milk mixture, stirring all the time. Slowly bring to the boil whilst stirring and continue stirring until the sauce thickens. Meanwhile, steam the cauliflower until just tender. Add the cooked cauliflower to the sauce and carefully mix in. Spoon into a warmed serving dish and garnish with chopped fresh parsley.

Broad bean and garlic purée *(serves 4)*

1¹/₂lb/675g shelled broad beans

2 tablespoons olive oil

2 garlic cloves, crushed

1 teaspoon dried oregano

1 teaspoon lemon juice

Steam the broad beans until tender, then allow to cool. Heat the oil and gently fry the garlic without browning. Remove from the heat. Slip the broad beans from their skins and discard the skins. Add the beans to the pan together with the oregano and lemon juice. Mix well, then mash or blend until smooth. Transfer to a baking dish, cover with foil and place in a preheated oven at 180°C/350°F/Gas mark 4 for 15 minutes until heated through.

SALADS

Italian salads contain an assortment of interesting and colourful leaves, such as lollo rosso, quattro stagioni, radicchio, chicory, young spinach, basil, curly endive, rocket and lambs lettuce, to name but a few. These leaves can be combined with other popular salad ingredients to create an endless variety of appetising dishes, which may be served either as a starter with crostini or as an accompaniment to main courses. Salads made with pasta, beans and lentils are also very popular. The classic dressing given here can be served with any type of salad.

Salad dressing

6 tablespoons olive oil

1 tablespoon white wine vinegar

1 tablespoon lemon juice

2 garlic cloves, crushed

2 tablespoons finely chopped fresh basil

black pepper

Whisk until well combined.

Margherita salad *(serves 4)*

8oz/225g tomatoes, chopped

3oz/75g pasta shells

1 avocado pear, peeled, stoned and diced

2oz/50g vegan 'mozzarella', diced

2 gherkins, thinly sliced

1 dessertspoon olive oil

1 dessertspoon white wine vinegar

1 teaspoon lemon juice

1 teaspoon balsamic vinegar

1 dessertspoon finely chopped fresh oregano

black pepper

quattro stagioni lettuce leaves

chopped walnuts

Cook the pasta shells until al dente, drain and rinse under cold running water. Drain well and put in a bowl with the tomatoes, gherkins and oregano. Mix the olive oil with the lemon juice and vinegars and pour over the salad. Season with black pepper and mix well, then carefully stir in the avocado and 'mozzarella'. Arrange some lettuce leaves on a serving plate and pile the salad on top. Garnish with chopped walnuts.

Rice salad *(serves 4/6)*

8oz/225g Italian brown rice

4oz/100g cooked borlotti beans

2oz/50g red pepper

2oz/50g green pepper

2oz/50g yellow pepper

2oz/50g cucumber

1 tablespoon finely chopped fresh parsley

1 tablespoon capers

black pepper

mixed salad leaves

dressing

2 tablespoons olive oil

2 dessertspoons white wine vinegar

1 dessertspoon lemon juice

2 garlic cloves, crushed

Cook the rice, drain and rinse under cold running water. Drain well and put in a mixing bowl with the borlotti beans. Finely chop the red, green and yellow peppers and the cucumber and add to the rice together with the parsley and capers. Season with black pepper and mix well. Whisk the dressing ingredients and spoon over the salad. Toss until well combined. Arrange some mixed salad leaves around the edge of a serving dish and spoon the rice salad in the middle. Cover and chill before serving.

Green lentil, pasta and pepper salad (*serves 4*)

2oz/50g green lentils

2oz/50g tiny pasta shapes

1oz/25g green pepper, finely chopped

1oz/25g yellow pepper, finely chopped

1oz/25g red pepper, finely chopped

2 spring onions, trimmed and finely sliced

2 tablespoons salsa verde

1 tomato, cut into thin wedges

Cook the lentils until tender, drain and put in a mixing bowl. Cook the pasta until al dente, then drain and rinse under cold running water. Drain well and add to the lentils together with the remaining ingredients apart from the tomato wedges. Mix thoroughly, transfer to a serving bowl and arrange the tomato wedges around the edge. Cover and chill for a couple of hours before serving.

Tomato and cucumber salad *(serves 4)*

8oz/225g tomatoes, finely sliced

cucumber slices

4 spring onions, trimmed and finely sliced

2 tablespoons olive oil

1 tablespoon red wine vinegar

1 garlic clove, crushed

black pepper

finely chopped fresh basil

curly endive leaves

Put some endive leaves on a serving plate. Arrange alternate slices of tomato and cucumber on the endive in a circular pattern and sprinkle the spring onions on top. Mix the olive oil with the vinegar and garlic and season with black pepper. Drizzle this dressing evenly over the salad and garnish with chopped fresh basil. Cover and chill.

Cauliflower and roasted red pepper salad *(serves 4)*

1lb/450g cauliflower, cut into florets

1 red pepper

1 tablespoon capers

8 green olives, halved

2 tablespoons olive oil

1 tablespoon white wine vinegar

1 garlic clove, crushed

1 tablespoon finely chopped fresh parsley

black pepper

Grill the red pepper all over until the skin chars and blisters. Allow to cool slightly, remove the skin and cut the flesh into thin slices. Steam the cauliflower for 5 minutes, then rinse under cold water. Drain well and put in a mixing bowl with the capers and olives. Mix the olive oil with the vinegar, garlic and parsley and pour over the salad, season with black pepper and toss well. Spoon the salad into a serving dish and arrange the pepper slices on top. Cover and chill before serving.

Mushroom and cannellini bean salad *(serves 4)*

8oz/225g button mushrooms, wiped and sliced

8oz/225g cooked cannellini beans

4 spring onions, trimmed and sliced

2 garlic cloves, crushed

2 tablespoons olive oil

2 dessertspoons lemon juice

2 tablespoons white wine

1 tablespoon finely chopped fresh parsley

black pepper

fresh parsley sprigs

Heat the oil in a pan and gently fry the garlic. Remove from the heat and add the lemon juice and wine, stirring briskly until well combined. Add the mushrooms and stir around until coated in the dressing. Now add the beans, spring onions and chopped parsley and season with black pepper. Toss well and put in a serving bowl. Garnish with parsley sprigs, cover and chill.

Roasted courgettes with red pesto salad *(serves 4)*

1¹/₂lb/675g courgettes

olive oil

2 rounded tablespoons red pesto

lollo rosso lettuce leaves

fresh basil leaves

Brush the courgettes with olive oil and bake whole in a preheated oven at 180°C/350°F/Gas mark 4 for 30-35 minutes until just tender. Allow to cool, then slice them. Add the red pesto and mix thoroughly. Arrange some lollo rosso lettuce leaves on a serving place and pile the salad on top. Garnish with fresh basil leaves.

Mixed bean salad *(serves 4)*

8oz/225g shelled broad beans

6oz/175g green beans, topped, tailed and cut into 1 inch/2.5cm lengths

6oz/175g cooked borlotti beans

4oz/100g tomatoes, skinned and finely chopped

1 dessertspoon olive oil

1 teaspoon balsamic vinegar

1 dessertspoon finely chopped fresh basil

black pepper

raddichio leaves

Steam the broad beans until tender. Cool under cold running water, drain well and remove the beans from their skins. Put them in a mixing bowl with the borlotti beans. Steam the green beans until just tender, rinse under cold running water, drain well and add to the other beans. Mix the olive oil with the balsamic vinegar, tomatoes and basil and season with black pepper. Add to the beans and toss thoroughly. Arrange some raddichio leaves on a serving plate and spoon the bean salad on top. Cover and chill before serving.

DESSERTS

With market stalls laden with fresh fruit, Italians are spoilt for choice when it comes to planning desserts. Fruit salads are naturally very popular, but Italians also have a passion for cream and desserts such as panna cotta, cassata and iced vanilla rice are favourites as well. Granitas are believed to have originated in Rome, but they are now eaten throughout the country. This simple and refreshing dessert is excellent for serving after a rich meal. Granitas are very versatile and can be made with any soft fruit that is in season, or simply with fruit juice.

Melon granita *(serves 6)*

> 1 medium-sized ripe melon (honeydew, cantaloupe or galia)
> 10 fl.oz/300ml hot water
> 2oz/50g granulated sugar

Stir the sugar in the water until dissolved, then allow to cool. Scoop the melon flesh out and put it in a blender, add the sugar water and blend until smooth. Pour into a shallow tray and freeze until just frozen. If the granita is too hard, leave it in the fridge for 30 minutes before serving.

Orange granita *(serves 6)*

> 20 fl.oz/600ml fresh orange juice
> 2 teaspoons agar agar
> 2 tablespoons demerara sugar

Dissolve the agar agar in the orange juice and add the sugar. Heat whilst stirring until just below boiling point. Pour into a shallow freezerproof tray and freeze until just frozen. Put in the fridge for 30 minutes before serving if it has become too solid.

Lemon and wine granita *(serves 6)*

4 fl.oz/125ml lemon juice

6 fl.oz/175ml water

8 fl.oz/225ml white wine

2 teaspoons agar agar

5oz/150g granulated sugar

Put the lemon juice, water and wine in a saucepan with the agar agar and stir until dissolved. Add the sugar and heat whilst stirring until just below boiling point. Pour the mixture into a shallow tray and freeze until just frozen. If it has become too hard, put in the fridge for 30 minutes before serving.

Chestnut purée with cream *(serves 4)*

15$^{1}/_{2}$oz/439g tin sweetened chestnut purée

2oz/50g soft brown sugar

2 tablespoons brandy

1 teaspoon lemon juice

vegan 'cream'

Put the chestnut purée, sugar, brandy and lemon juice in a bowl and mix thoroughly. Sieve the purée into a serving dish, forming a mound. Serve with some vegan 'cream'.

Iced vanilla rice *(serves 4)*

A deliciously creamy, rich vanilla ice cream that is thought to have originated in Sicily.

> 2oz/50g round grain pudding rice
>
> 1oz/25g granulated sugar
>
> 10 fl.oz/300ml soya milk
>
> 9 fl.oz/250ml vegan 'cream'
>
> 1 vanilla pod

Put the rice, sugar, soya milk and vanilla pod in a pan. Stir well and bring to the boil. Cover and simmer very gently until the milk has been absorbed. Stir occasionally to prevent sticking. Remove the vanilla pod, allow to cool and leave in the fridge until cold.

Add the 'cream' and mix thoroughly. Spoon into a freezerproof container, cover and freeze. After 1 hour, remove from the freezer and stir well. Put back in the freezer and freeze until just frozen. Should it have become too hard, thaw at room temperature for 30 minutes. Serve scoops of the ice cream with fresh fruit salad or a fruit purée.

Panna cotta with strawberry purée *(serves 4)*

> 18 fl.oz/500ml vegan 'cream'
>
> 1oz/25g caster sugar
>
> 1 teaspoon vanilla essence
>
> 2 tablespoons soya milk
>
> 2 tablespoons orange juice
>
> 2 rounded teaspoons agar agar
>
> **purée**
>
> 12oz/350g strawberries, chopped
>
> 1 tablespoon caster sugar
>
> 2 tablespoons orange juice
>
> 1 dessertspoon balsamic vinegar

4oz/100g strawberries, halved

Heat the 'cream', caster sugar and vanilla essence gently whilst stirring until just below boiling point, then remove from the heat. Put the soya milk, orange juice and agar agar in a pan and stir until the agar dissolves. Heat slowly until just below boiling point. Remove from the heat and add the 'cream' a little at a time, stirring briskly before adding more to avoid lumps. Pass the mixture through a fine sieve, then pour it into 4 5fl.oz/150ml moulds. Cover and keep in the fridge for a few hours until set.

Put the chopped strawberries, sugar and orange juice in a saucepan and gently heat until the strawberries soften. Pour into a blender with the balsamic vinegar and blend until smooth. Sieve the purée to remove the seeds, then put in the fridge for a few hours.

Carefully turn out the panna cottas onto serving plates. Spoon the purée around the edge and garnish with the strawberry halves.

Cassata *(serves 8)*

Many versions of this recipe appear throughout Italy. This one is easy to make, using vegan ice cream. You need to work quickly so that the ice cream doesn't thaw too much , so it is a good idea to have all the ingredients ready for mixing in before starting.

2 x 25 fl.oz/750ml cartons vegan vanilla ice cream

2oz/50g glacé cherries, washed, dried and chopped

1oz/25g mixed peel, finely chopped

1oz/25g glacé ginger, finely chopped

1oz/25g vegan chocolate, chopped into 'chips'

1oz/25g hazelnuts, chopped and toasted

1 tablespoon brandy

1 rounded teaspoon cocoa powder

1oz/25g almond macaroons (see page 114), crushed

1/2oz/15g vegan chocolate, grated

¹/₂oz/15g flaked almonds, broken

Line a 7 inch/18cm diameter loose-bottomed cake tin with foil or cling film. Put two-thirds of the ice cream into one mixing bowl and the remaining third into another one. Quickly mash the larger quantity and add the glacé cherries, mixed peel and ginger. Mix well, then spread half of this mixture into the base of the tin. Mix the cocoa powder with the brandy until smooth and add this to the other bowl of ice cream together with the hazelnuts and chocolate chips. Stir well and spoon evenly into the tin. Top with the remaining ice cream and press down firmly.

Mix the crushed macaroons with the grated chocolate and broken almonds. Sprinkle this evenly over the ice cream and press in lightly with the back of a spoon. Cover and freeze for a few hours until set. Carefully remove from the tin and cut into wedges to serve.

Fruit salad

Choose a selection of fruit from strawberries, apricots, peaches, figs, grapes, melon, oranges, plums and pears. Allow 4-6oz/100-175g of prepared fruit per person and sprinkle any fruit that might discolour with lemon juice. Add a little fruit juice, and a dash of sparkling wine or fruit liqueur for special occasions.

Stuffed baked peaches *(serves 4)*

4 firm peaches

4oz/100g almond macaroons (see page 114), crushed

2oz/50g mixed cake fruit, chopped

1 rounded tablespoon golden syrup

flaked almonds

Cut the peaches in half and remove the stones. Scoop out a little of the flesh to make the hollow a bit bigger. Chop the removed flesh and add to the crushed macaroons and mixed fruit. Heat the golden syrup in a saucepan until runny, remove from the heat and stir in the fruit mixture. Stir well, then fill each peach half with some of the filling, shaping it neatly on top. Put the stuffed peaches in a baking dish and sprinkle with flaked almonds. Bake in a preheated oven at 180°C/350°F/Gas mark 4 for 25 minutes until just tender.

Apricot and hazelnut tart *(serves 4)*

base

4oz/100g plain flour

2oz/50g hazelnuts, grated and toasted

2oz/50g vegan margarine

2 tablespoons soya milk

topping

12oz/350g fresh apricots, halved and stoned

1 rounded tablespoon demerara sugar

1 tablespoon fresh orange juice

flaked hazelnuts

Add the grated hazelnuts to the flour and rub in the margarine, stir in the soya milk and mix thoroughly. Spoon the mixture into a lined and greased 7 inch/18cm diameter flan tin and press down firmly and evenly. Prick the top all over and bake blind in a preheated oven at 180°C/350°F/Gas mark 4 for 5 minutes.

Put the apricots, sugar and orange juice in a saucepan and cook for about 3 minutes whilst stirring carefully. Remove from the heat and drain. Arrange the apricot halves in a circular pattern on top of the base. Sprinkle with flaked hazelnuts and return to the oven for 35 minutes. Serve either hot or cold.

Apple and almond cake (serves 8)

1lb/450g apples, peeled and cored

8oz/225g self raising flour

4oz/100g vegan margarine

2oz/50g demerara sugar

2oz/50g ground almonds

1oz/25g soya flour

1 rounded tablespoon golden syrup

4 tablespoons soya milk

1 teaspoon almond essence

topping

1 dessertspoon golden syrup

flaked almonds

Put the margarine, sugar and tablespoonful of golden syrup in a large pan and heat gently until melted. Remove from the heat and stir in the ground almonds and flour. Finely chop half the apples and add to the mixture. Whisk the soya flour with the soya milk and almond essence, add and mix thoroughly. Spoon into a greased loose-bottomed 7 inch/18cm diameter cake tin. Press down firmly and evenly.

Thinly slice the remaining apples and arrange the slices in a circular pattern on top of the cake. Heat the dessertspoonful of golden syrup until runny, then brush this evenly over the apple slices. Sprinkle with flaked almonds and cover loosely with foil. Bake in a preheated oven at 180°C/350°F/Gas mark 4 for 1 hour. Remove the foil and bake for 5-10 minutes more until golden. Leave in the tin for 10 minutes, then turn the cake out onto a wire rack to get cold.

BAKING

Italian breads are quite unlike those of other countries, mainly because they are made with olive oil and flavoured with herbs, Parmesan, olives and other savoury additions. In Italy, bread is treated with great respect and it is always served with every meal.

Almonds and hazelnuts feature often in cakes and biscuits. It was the Italians who invented amaretti (almond macaroons), which are now famous throughout the world.

Onion and sage focaccia *(makes 2)*

1½lb/675g plain flour

1 sachet easy-blend yeast

4 tablespoons olive oil

1 onion, peeled and finely chopped

1 tablespoon finely chopped fresh sage

1 teaspoon salt

approx. 12 fl.oz/350ml warm water

extra olive oil

Heat 1 dessertspoonful of olive oil and gently fry the onion until softened. Put the flour, yeast and salt in a bowl and mix. Add the onion and sage and remaining olive oil and stir thoroughly. Gradually add the water until a soft dough is formed. Turn out onto a floured board and knead well. Return to the bowl, cover with an oiled piece of cling film and leave in a warm place for 1 hour until risen. Turn out onto a floured board and knead again. Divide the dough into 2 equal pieces and put each one in an oiled 8 inch/20cm diameter flan tin. Press the dough out to fill the tins. Cover with oiled cling film and leave in a warm place for 30 minutes. Using your fingertips, make deep dimples all over the top of the dough. Brush with olive oil and bake in a preheated oven at 200°C/400°F/Gas mark 6 for approximately 15 minutes until golden brown. Turn out onto a wire rack and allow to cool.

Olive and basil focaccia *(makes 2)*

1½lb/675g plain flour

1 sachet easy-blend yeast

4 tablespoons olive oil

1 teaspoon salt

10 black olives, finely chopped

10 green olives, halved

1 tablespoon finely chopped fresh basil

approx. 12 fl.oz/350ml warm water

extra olive oil

Mix the flour, yeast and salt in a large bowl. Add the basil, chopped black olives and 4 tablespoonfuls of olive oil and mix well. Gradually add the water until a soft dough forms. Turn this out onto a floured board and knead. Return to the bowl and cover with a piece of oiled cling film, then leave in a warm place for 1 hour to rise. Turn out onto a floured board and knead again. Divide the dough into 2 equal pieces and roll or shape each piece into an oval of about ½ inch/1cm thick. Put these on an oiled baking sheet, cover with oiled cling film and leave in a warm place for 30 minutes. Press 10 green olive halves into the top of each oval and brush the dough with olive oil. Bake in a preheated oven at 200°C/400°F/Gas mark 6 for about 15 minutes until browned. Put on a wire rack to cool.

Walnut and maize bread

1lb/450g plain flour

4oz/100g maizemeal

3oz/75g walnuts, finely chopped

1 sachet easy-blend yeast

3 tablespoons olive oil

1 teaspoon salt

approx. 15 fl.oz/450ml warm water

extra olive oil

Put the flour, maizemeal, walnuts, yeast and salt in a bowl and mix. Add the 3 tablespoonfuls of olive oil and stir well. Gradually add the water, until the mixture binds together and a soft dough forms. Turn out onto a floured board and knead thoroughly. Return the dough to the bowl, cover it with a piece of oiled cling film and leave it to rise for 1 hour in a warm place. Knead again, then shape the dough into a ball and put this in a 7 inch/18cm diameter greased flan tin. Cut a cross in the top of the dough. Cover with oiled cling film and leave in a warm place for 45 minutes. Bake in a preheated oven at 200°C/400°F/Gas mark 6 for 30 minutes, then invert the bread onto a cooling tray and remove the tin. Return the bread to the oven upside down for 5 minutes, until golden and hollow sounding when tapped. Put on a wire rack to get cold.

Herby Parmesan breadsticks *(makes 36)*

1lb/450g plain flour

2 teaspoons easy-blend yeast

1 teaspoon salt

1 teaspoon dried sage

1 teaspoon dried rosemary

1 teaspoon dried oregano

2 tablespoons vegan 'Parmesan'

3 tablespoons olive oil

1 garlic clove, crushed

approx. 10 fl.oz/300ml warm water

Put the flour, yeast, salt, herbs, 'Parmesan' and garlic in a mixing bowl and stir together. Mix in the oil, then gradually add the water until a soft dough forms. Turn out onto a floured board and knead. Return to the bowl, cover with a piece of oiled cling film and leave in a warm place for 1 hour to rise. Turn the dough out onto a floured board and knead again. Divide it into 36 equal pieces and roll each piece into a stick of about 8 inches/20cm. Put the sticks on an oiled baking sheet and leave for 30 minutes in a warm place. Bake in a preheated oven at 200°C/400°F/Gas mark 6 for about 20 minutes until crisp and golden. Serve warm or cold.

Sun-dried tomato and oregano rolls *(makes 12)*

1½lb/675g plain flour

2oz/50g sun-dried tomatoes, finely chopped

1 sachet easy-blend yeast

4 tablespoons olive oil

1 dessertspoon sun-dried tomato paste

1 tablespoon dried oregano

1 teaspoon salt

approx. 15 fl.oz/450ml warm water

extra olive oil

Soak the sun-dried tomatoes in the 4 tablespoonfuls of olive oil overnight. Stir the flour, yeast, oregano and salt together in a large bowl, add the soaked tomatoes and the remaining oil and mix thoroughly. Dissolve the tomato paste in the water and gradually add to the mixture until a soft dough forms. Turn this out onto a floured board and knead well, then return to the bowl, cover with a piece of oiled cling firm and put in a warm place for 1 hour. Knead the dough again, then divide it into 12 equal pieces. Roll each piece into a round in the palm of the hand. Arrange 9 rounds in a circle on a greased baking sheet, put the remaining 3 in the centre and squeeze the whole shape together so that all the rounds are touching and no gaps remain. Cover with oiled cling film and leave in a warm place for 1 hour to rise. Brush the top with olive oil and bake in a preheated oven at 200°C/400°F/Gas mark 6 for about 20 minutes, until golden brown and hollow-sounding when tapped underneath. Transfer to a wire rack and cut into the 12 rolls when cold.

Panforte *(serves 10)*

This richly spiced, flat, chewy 'cake' is a speciality from Siena and there are many variations. It is traditionally served in thin slices with coffee or as a dessert.

6oz/175g cut mixed peel

3oz/75g hazelnuts, grated

3oz/75g almonds, ground

2oz/50g plain flour

1oz/25g demerara sugar

1oz/25g vegan margarine

½oz/15g cocoa powder

2 rounded tablespoons golden syrup

2 tablespoons soya milk

½ teaspoon ground cinnamon

½ teaspoon grated nutmeg

¼ teaspoon ground cloves

Put the grated hazelnuts and ground almonds into a shallow baking tin and toast until golden, stirring frequently to prevent burning.

Bring the margarine, sugar and golden syrup to the boil, then remove from the heat and stir in the nuts and mixed peel. Add the sifted flour, cocoa and spices together with the soya milk and mix thoroughly. Spoon the mixture into a lined and greased 8 inch/20cm diameter loose-bottomed flan tin, pressing it down firmly and evenly, and bake in a preheated oven at 170°C/325°F/Gas mark 3 for 30 minutes. Turn out onto a wire rack and allow to cool. Cut into thin wedges.

Almond macaroons *(makes 30)*

3oz/75g ground almonds

3oz/75g maizemeal

2oz/50g demerara sugar

1½oz/40g vegan margarine, melted

1oz/25g soya flour

1 teaspoon almond essence

4 fl.oz/125ml soya milk

Put the ground almonds, maizemeal, sugar and soya flour in a bowl and mix well. Stir the almond essence into the melted margarine and add to the dry ingredients. Mix thoroughly, then add the soya milk and combine until a soft dough forms. Spoon this into a piping bag and pipe 30 small rounds of the mixture on a greased and floured baking sheet. Bake in a preheated oven at 180°C/350°F/Gas mark 4 for 15-18 minutes until golden brown. Leave on the baking sheet for 5 minutes, then carefully put the macaroons on a wire rack.

Chocolate almond biscuits *(makes 20)*

4oz/100g ground almonds

2oz/50g plain flour

2oz/50g demerara sugar

½oz/15g soya flour

¼oz/7g cocoa powder

1oz/25g vegan margarine, melted

4 tablespoons soya milk

½ teaspoon almond essence

20 almond halves

Stir the ground almonds, sugar, flours and cocoa together. Mix the almond essence with the melted margarine and add, together with the soya milk. Combine thoroughly until everything binds together. Take heaped teaspoonfuls of the mixture and roll into balls in the palm of the hand. Flatten each ball into a biscuit shape and put it on a greased and floured baking sheet. Press an almond half into the top of each biscuit and bake in a preheated oven at 180°C/350°F/Gas mark 4 for 20 minutes. Carefully transfer to a wire rack and allow to cool.

Chocolate, walnut and raisin cake *(serves 8)*

4oz/100g plain flour

3oz/75g raisins, chopped

3oz/75g vegan margarine

2oz/50g walnuts, ground

2oz/50g demerara sugar

2oz/50g breadcrumbs

1oz/25g soya flour

3 fl.oz/75ml water

3 tablespoons rum

1 rounded tablespoon cocoa powder

6 fl.oz/175ml soya milk

filling

4oz/100g vegan 'cream cheese'

1 dessertspoon demerara sugar

1 dessertspoon cocoa powder

topping

3oz/75g vegan chocolate bar, broken

8 walnut halves

Soak the raisins in the rum for an hour. Cream the margarine with the sugar in a mixing bowl. Whisk the soya flour with the water until smooth and add to the bowl with the sifted cocoa. Stir in the soaked raisins and remaining rum together with the ground walnuts. Add the sifted flour, breadcrumbs and soya milk and mix thoroughly. Divide the mixture between 2 lined and greased 7 inch/18cm diameter flan tins. Spread out it evenly and bake in a preheated oven at 180°C/350°F/Gas mark 4 for 35 minutes. Allow to cool in the tins for 10 minutes, then turn out onto a wire rack to get cold.

Mix the filling ingredients until smooth and spread evenly onto one half of each of the cakes. Sandwich the two halves together. Melt the chocolate bar in a bowl over a pan of boiling water. Cover the top and sides of the cake with the chocolate, press the walnut halves into the top and refrigerate until set. Cut into wedges to serve. This cake should be stored in the fridge.

Florentines *(makes approx. 24)*

4oz/100g self raising flour

4oz/100g mixed cake fruit, finely chopped

2oz/50g vegan margarine

1oz/25g walnuts, finely chopped

1 rounded tablespoon golden syrup

1 tablespoon soya milk

¼ teaspoon grated nutmeg

2oz/50g dark vegan chocolate, melted

Heat the golden syrup and margarine gently until melted. Remove from the heat and add the remaining ingredients apart from the chocolate. Mix thoroughly, then take rounded teaspoonfuls and put them on a greased baking sheet. Flatten and neaten each pile into a round biscuit shape. Bake in a preheated oven at 180°C/350°F/Gas mark 4 for about 10 minutes until golden brown. Leave on the baking sheet for 10 minutes, then carefully put on a wire rack. When cold, spread the flat side of each biscuit with melted chocolate and allow it to set.

Hazelnut biscuits *(makes approx. 16)*

4oz/100g plain flour

2oz/50g hazelnuts, grated and lightly toasted

2oz/50g vegan margarine

1oz/25g demerara sugar

1 rounded tablespoon golden syrup

Cream the margarine with the golden syrup and sugar. Work in the hazelnuts and flour until everything binds together. Take rounded teaspoonfuls of the mixture and roll into balls in the palm of the hand. Flatten each ball into a round and place on a greased baking sheet. Prick the biscuits with a fork and bake them in a preheated oven at 170°C/325°F/Gas mark 3 for 10-12 minutes until browned. Carefully transfer to a wire rack.

Almond and maizemeal slices *(makes 12)*

3oz/75g plain flour

3oz/75g maizemeal

2oz/50g ground almonds

2oz/50g vegan margarine

1½oz/40g demerara sugar

½ teaspoon almond essence

5 tablespoons soya milk

Cream the margarine with the sugar and almond essence. Work in the ground almonds and maizemeal, then add the flour and soya milk. Mix until a soft dough forms. Turn out onto a floured board and shape into an oblong of about 7 x 3½ inches/18 x 9cm. Cut this into 12 equal slices. Turn the slices over and make an indent along the length of each slice with a finger. Put the slices on a greased baking sheet and bake in a preheated oven at 180°C/350°F/Gas mark 4 for about 20 minutes until golden brown. Carefully transfer to a wire rack and leave to cool.

Pane cioccolata

An unusual chocolate-flavoured bread, which is served in thin slices with coffee.

>1lb/450g plain flour
>2oz/50g demerara sugar
>2oz/50g vegan margarine, melted
>1oz/25g cocoa powder
>1 sachet easy-blend yeast
>approx. 8 fl.oz/225ml soya milk, warmed
>2oz/50g vegan chocolate, finely chopped

Mix the flour, sugar, cocoa powder and yeast. Stir in the melted margarine, then gradually add the soya milk until a soft dough forms. Turn out onto a board and knead. Return the dough to the bowl, cover with a piece of greased cling film and leave to rise for 1 hour in a warm place. Work the chopped chocolate pieces into the dough whilst kneading again. Place the dough in an 8 inch/20cm diameter baking tin and put in a warm place for 30 minutes. Bake in a preheated oven at 200°C/400°F/Gas mark 6 for about 20 minutes, until the loaf sounds hollow when tapped underneath. Turn it out onto a wire rack to cool. Cut into slices and spread with vegan margarine to serve.